Raising a Norwegia

CW01629720

Guidebook how to educ

A book for cat babies, kittens and young cats

Expertengruppe Verlag

The contents of this book have been compiled with the greatest care. However, no guarantee can be provided for its accuracy, completeness and topicality. The contents of this book are a representation of the author's personal experiences and opinions. No responsibility or liability is accepted for counter-productive exercise of the recommendations or mistakes made by the reader. No guarantee of success is implied. The author does not accept responsibility for the success or otherwise of the methods described in this book.

All the content presented here is exclusively intended to be neutral information and in no way meant to be recommendations or advertisements of the methods described or mentioned within. This book does not claim to be complete, nor can the topicality or accuracy of the information offered be guaranteed. This work is not intended to replace expert advice or care from a veterinary surgeon. The author and the publisher are not liable for any inconvenience or damages resulting from use of this book.

Raising a Norwegian Forest Cat

Guidebook how to educate a Norwegian Forest Kitten

A book for cat babies, kittens and young cats

Expertengruppe Verlag

CONTENTS

ABOUT THE AUTHOR

Susanne Herzog is a true animal lover – to be more precise she is a cat lover, not surprisingly because she grew up in a household full of cats.

From an early age she developed her love of animals by helping out regularly in an animal shelter. For the first time she became aware of the darker side of keeping animals – with neglected, traumatised and practically unsocialised animals. This aroused her interest and she began to analyse how these things could happen. But rather than try to just analyse the reasons for it, it was much more important for her to find out how the majority of problems could be avoided in the first place. Based on that, she developed methods to help animals with acute behavioural problems to settle into a better and more normal life.

Susanne Herzog is not content just to help cats in the shelter, in which she is still working on a voluntary basis, she also gives seminars for stressed cat owners several times a year. The experiences gained in her work and the feedback she received from participants of her courses, gave her the idea of expanding the accessibility of her wide-ranging knowledge to a larger group of people in the form of a book.

Her aim is to help cat owners to set the right course between human and cat, from the very beginning, so that they can live happy and enriched lives together. She wants to avoid people from making the mistakes right at the beginning which can lead to bigger problems, causing the cat to be taken to a shelter.

After a long process of research, writing and correction, this guidebook emerged. In addition to general directions on raising cats, particular attention is given in this book to the Norwegian Forest Cat. It is intended to give future Norwegian Forest Cat owners a guide to getting the difficult task of raising your cat right at the first attempt. Every cat is worth the effort of avoiding the mistakes which so many unknowledgeable cat owners make at the beginning. Over the years, Susanne Herzog has seen that such mistakes often lead to the cat being taken to a shelter, and it is hoped that the readers of this book can be spared from that.

Those of you who follow the tips in this guidebook can be sure to have many years of pleasure together with this exceptional companion.

PREFACE

Congratulations on making an excellent choice in welcoming your Norwegian Forest Cat into your home. In addition, you have chosen to buy this guidebook, thereby making a second good decision.

A young cat is a bundle of energy. It is able to capture everyone's heart with its clumsiness, fluffy fur and endless trust in you, its owner. Your little Norwegian Forest Cat will fulfil you every day and soon you will not be able to imagine life without it.

Before you read the following pages, you should know what to expect in this book. This guidebook will not change your little bundle of fun into a well-behaved cat overnight. It will, however, show you some shortcuts to success. And most importantly, purely reading this will not change anything. Your success depends entirely upon yourself.

This guidebook will give you all the information you need, not only to find a friend for life but also to be able to raise a fear-free, happy, self-confident and well-behaved Norwegian Forest Cat. This book is based on gentle pet-parenting methods whilst maintaining fixed rules, applying constant repetitions and having endless patience.

It will not always be easy for you to remain consistent, particularly when looking into those big, sweet cat eyes, but I guarantee that it is worth it in the end. If you follow the methods described in this book, not only you will profit from it but also your Norwegian Forest Cat, who will be able to live a fulfilled, safe and free life.

Are you committed to investing a lot of time and above all, love, in your Norwegian Forest Cat, not only in the first few weeks but for its whole life?

Then you have made the right choice and you can read the next pages!

From my heart, I wish you both much success and good luck.

Please do not be surprised if I always address cats in the neutral form in this guidebook, this is done for better readability.

- Chapter 1 -

What you need to know about your Norwegian Forest Cat

The Norwegian Forest Cat is a very special breed of cat, which is very different from many others. Training cats involves many elements which are the same for all breeds. However, every breed has its particular characteristics and character which make it unique. It is exactly these characteristics which are important in raising cats.

Some cat-parenting elements are much more difficult, easier or more important for your Norwegian Forest Cat than for example a Persian cat and I will therefore point out the differences throughout the book, wherever they occur. Often the methods for raising cats are the same for all breeds but I will let you know if there is something which you need to watch particularly with your Norwegian Forest Cat. But firstly, it is important that you get to know your Norwegian Forest Cat and its characteristics.

Those who are looking for a feral-looking but still people-loving, friendly and cuddly cat will find exactly what they are looking for in the Norwegian Forest Cat. This cat belongs to one of the few "natural" cat breeds. That means that it has not been specifically bred by humans, but has developed through natural selection. It is perfectly suited to the conditions existing in Norway. Its fur is very dense and water-resistant which protects it during the cold winters in Scandinavia. It possesses heavy tufting between its toes, which allows it to move over snow without sinking.

It was not until the 1930s before breeders intentionally began to preserve the genes of this breed, as wild cats often mated with short-haired housecats. They were first recognised by the international federation of cat registries, FIFe in 1977.

Apart from the Norwegian Forest Cat's abundant, fluffy fur, it is conspicuous because of its ears, which have small, lynx-like fur bundles on them. Its fur is not only water-resistant, but also provides it with a bib, neck ruff and britches in the winter months. The Norwegian Forest Cat grows a particularly dense undercoat in these places to protect it from the cold winters.

On closer inspection, you can see that its hind legs are longer than its front legs. This is another sign that it is suited to its environment. Longer hind legs give it enormous leaping power, which is a great advantage when hunting.

Despite all these wonderful abilities, which enable it to live in the wild, the Norwegian Forest Cat has developed into a very popular house cat. One reason for this is surely to be found in its character, not only in its beauty. It is sometimes called the "gentle giant" because it is good-natured and affectionate. These are truly "cuddly animals" which demand the attention and petting they want from their humans. They are extremely playful and very sociable. For this reason, it is not advisable to keep them alone or alone from their humans, for any long periods of time.

Because of its size, love of hunting games and ability to make big leaps, you are advised not to keep your Norwegian Forest Cat as a purely house cat. It would love a secured garden or balcony with enough possibilities to climb and play, particularly if it is able to play with other cats. It is also willing to accept other small animals and even dogs as playmates.

Its quiet nature, robustness and playfulness makes it an ideal playmate for children. It is extremely tolerant and seldom skittish. It is important that it is well-socialised in its youth and that the children are not too rough with it. It is hardly ever aggressive and prefers to flee when it gets too much for it.

Your Norwegian Forest Cat is very intelligent, so you should plan to spend time every day playing, hunting and training it right from the beginning. You will probably need a lot of cat toys in order to offer it the diversity it needs.

If your Norwegian Forest Cat does not get enough attention to occupy it, it soon becomes bored. It does not like being left alone for several hours a day and it would lead to your cat finding its own ways to occupy itself, which could include emptying all the cupboards out or “redecorating” your home. If you are thinking of getting a second cat, you must ensure that it is also an active and playful one. Quiet breeds, like the Persian cat or the British Shorthair would not go well with your Norwegian Forest Cat as they have different needs which need to be fulfilled.

If you have not yet decided on getting a Norwegian Forest Cat but are thinking about buying one, here is a tip for you: Go to a reputable breeder and find out everything you can about this animal and its parents. Your Norwegian Forest Cat will live an average of 12 - 15years, so it is important that it comes from a healthy and socialised breeding source and will not have a difficult life from birth because of overbreeding. Take a good look at how the breeder looks after his cats and if this matches up with the methods you will read about in this book. A cat which has been traumatised from an early age requires an enormous retraining programme and most cat owners are not able or willing to do that. A reputable breeder will always be able to show you the pedigree of the animal. You should not be able to see the same ancestor appear twice in it, in order to avoid inbreeding problems from the start. Even if it seems extreme, a serious breeder will often ask for around 700 -

1000 USD for a Norwegian Forest Cat. Anything below that should make you suspicious, as it could be the result of a so-called propagator. These people are less interested in appropriate breeding techniques and socialising their animals.

Take a good look at the cat babies, their parents and the breeder before you make your purchase, so that your happy life with your Norwegian Forest Cat is not fraught with difficulties from the beginning.

Of course, you can take a Norwegian Forest Cat from the animal shelter any time. This not only a very noble and exemplary gesture, but you will also be able to give a cat the chance of a fulfilled and happy life. However, not everyone is able take home an animal shelter cat without problems. This could be a health problem of the cat which could cost a lot of money on medical costs for the rest of the cat's life, or perhaps the poor little thing has already been subject to some trauma which could cause behavioural difficulties, making it difficult to place with a family or working person.

It is possible that neither of those things are present but the chances are higher with a cat from the animal shelter than with a cat from a reputable breeder. So, you need to be clear which risks are involved and speak about these with the animal shelter in detail. If you feel up to the job, it is great that you are able to give a shelter cat a new home! In the case of your Norwegian Forest Cat, it probably means that you need to be more patient in its upbringing and plan in more repeats in order to work through old experiences and over-write behavioural patterns. But with the right attitude, and clear commitment you will also be able to do it, I am sure of that.

You will find a quick summary about the Norwegian Forest Cat breed on the following pages. In addition, you will find a checklist of everything you need to take into consideration when you are buying your cat in the chapter called "Checklist for the start".

PROFILE OF THE NORWEGIAN FOREST CAT

Photo	
Origin	Norway
Size	Large to very large Head to tail length: up to 130 cm Shoulder height: up to 45 cm
Weight	Female: 4 – 8 kg Male: 5 – 9.5 kg
Build	The body is very muscular but also elegant. Its body and legs are long.
Head Shape	Its head is triangular and it has a strong chin line. Its forehead is slightly rounded.
Eyes	The eyes are large and oval. All colours are allowed.

Fur and Colouring	The fur is mid-length, dense and water-repellent with a woolly undercoat. In winter it has a dense neck ruff. All colours, except lilac, chocolate, cinnamon and fawn are allowed.
Coat Care	Regular brushing is advisable because of its hair length, to avoid matting. It should be brushed weekly during the moulting season.
Character	It is friendly, intelligent and attentive. It has a stable character and a strong need for exercise.
Special Characteristics	It has heavy tufting between its toes, which allows it to move over the snow without sinking.

- Chapter 2 -

Essentials for Raising a Cat

There are numerous books about raising cats and even more opinions. Nearly every cat owner does it differently and you will already have received many tips from friends, relatives and other cat owners. It would not be surprising if you were wondering whether to take cat training so seriously. Cat training methods are not really considered as important as they are with dogs. After all, is it really important that our little darlings do obey as well as Lassie did?

The answer is clearly “YES”! Even cat training is unbelievably important.

At this point I must mention that I do not mean that your little Norwegian Forest Cat has to learn to give paw or turn three times on the spot at your signal. It is not about that at all and there will be nothing in this book like that.

Let me explain it like this: You probably do not live like a hermit, somewhere far from anywhere in the Canadian wilderness. You probably live in a normal village or town and lead a normal life, where your cat does not have so much free room. In addition, there are the various distractions in our environment, such as "strangers" entering your home, or you not being home 24/7. Besides that, you most probably would prefer to live with your cat in peaceful harmony and have a certain standard of order and cleanliness, do you not? I assume furthermore that you would prefer your cat to use a cat toilet instead of a plant pot and that you do not want it to turn your home upside down in the night and regularly sharpen its claws on your couch. It would also be nice if you do not have to guard your open foods or that visitors do not cause your Norwegian Forest Cat to become intolerably stressed.

It is important that your cat learns from you how to behave in our modern world, so that you can enjoy life together and, at the same time, be able to have a certain amount of freedom. For example, it should not be afraid of noises, such as the vacuum cleaner or the rubbish collector. It should not worry about people, such as workmen, entering your house or new things around the house, like carpets. It should not become aggressive and must be able to rely on you completely.

If you bring up your cat well, your lives together will be much more pleasant and relaxed. Your cat will be less stressed and in turn will be able to enjoy more freedom. This means that it can move more freely outside of your four walls. You will be able to leave your house without fear of what it might be destroying or where it will urinate this time. Many owners underestimate how useful it is for cats to be raised well and will never come to enjoy how close, trustworthy and fulfilling having a well-trained cat can be.

If you do not want to belong to that group of people, you will learn everything you need to know about how to make your lives together as fulfilling as possible in the pages to follow.

TRAINING CATS – IMPOSSIBLE?

Since you have bought my book, it seems you are seriously thinking of training your young cat. If you talk about this – very reasonable – idea, most people will be astonished and tell you that you cannot train cats.

Naturally, this people are not completely wrong. Most cats are missing the so-called "will to please". Moreover, what many like about cats is their high level of self-confidence and strong will. Your cat should not lose any of these characteristics. Quite the contrary, but it should learn that there are rules in your house which it has to follow.

You do not need to take to heart accusations of those people who say that this is not an appropriate way to keep cats. Anyone who has been involved intensively with cats knows that even cats have certain rules among themselves, which they all follow, so that they can live peacefully together. A cat mother will make it very clear to her kittens what is allowed and what is not. The young cats learn quickly when they have gone too far.

You hear the excuse that cats are impossible to train or that it is not appropriate, mostly from those people who shy away from making the effort involved. Naturally, you need to know that training a Norwegian Forest Cat will take a lot of time, work and energy, but it will be worth it. To be exact, training cats is more about training the behaviour of people so that the cat learns to behave accordingly. In most cases of "problem cats" that I know of, the bulk of these problems lay with the behaviour of the owners, who subconsciously allow the cat's behaviour to become a problem. I want to help you to avoid doing that.

You need to know that cats usually learn very quickly what they are allowed to do and what not. However, due to their independence and their lack of "will to please", it does not always make sense for them to permanently obey you, which drives some cat owners crazy. Using the positive reinforcement that you will learn in this book, you will understand how to make it in their interest to obey certain commands. You will see that the amount of ignored commands will decrease until they will hopefully stop happening altogether.

Please be clear from the start that there are some things which your cat will not, or cannot learn because it is not in its nature. What do I mean by that? As an example, the Norwegian Forest Cat does not scratch your new couch to make you angry but solely because it is marking its territory and that the same time sharpening its claws. It just doesn't know that you do not like it scratching the new couch. Also, it does not run riot at night in your home to deliberately stop you from sleeping, but it is just following its own nature.

You will not be able to get rid of the examples I just mentioned completely by using any kind of training methods because it is in a cat's nature. In fact, that is not even the aim of my trainings. We do not want to change the basic character of your cat, but to improve the quality of you two living together and make things simpler. The real aim is not to get rid of the unacceptable behaviour completely but to channel it into an acceptable direction.

You need to be clear about what is acceptable behaviour from your Norwegian Forest Cat and should not expect too much. It is important that you give it enough freedom to be able to live its life in an appropriate way for its breed, despite your training. If the cat does not get enough training, the result is usually that you have a bored, frustrated animal at home, which often displays unacceptable behaviour. Unfortunately, many owners tend to give their animals too much freedom, which makes the problem even worse.

It may sound strange but even those self-reliant, headstrong feline pets prefer it when they are given clear guidance. Of course, they would never admit it, but (as with us humans) it is really better to be given boundaries, combined with positive reinforcement.

A cat which knows what it is allowed to do, and what not, leads a more relaxed life than that of its untrained counterparts. For this reason, and many others, I can confirm, without a doubt, that training a cat is not impossible. It is up to the owner whether or not he is prepared to put in the work.

Special Characteristics of your Norwegian Forest Cat

You are lucky with your Norwegian Forest Cat that this breed shows a relatively keen interest in maintaining an active interaction with you as the owner. This can be a great advantage, as it could make it much easier for you to motivate your Norwegian Forest Cat than it is for owners of other breeds of cat. Generally, it is willing to take part in any activity that you offer it. Due to its intelligence, it is able to understand what is going on and imitate what it sees very quickly.

On the other hand, this gives you a great responsibility. Your Norwegian Forest Cat does not like to be alone and, when you are there, it likes to interact with you. You need to be aware that your cat is not a cuddly toy to be stroked when you feel like it and which otherwise sits quietly in the corner and waits. If you do not give it the attention it needs, your cat will certainly let you know it. Should it not get enough attention and stimulation over a longer period of time, it could lead to your Norwegian Forest Cat starting to show behavioural abnormalities.

You will find out what you need to know about the inner-predator of your Norwegian Forest Cat over the next few chapters, so that this does not happen to you.

THE INNER-PREDATOR

This may sound incredible, but we humans have only been living closely together with cats for a short time. In contrast to dogs, which have been living with humans for hundreds, if not thousands, of years, the house cat as we know it today has only been around for about 150 years. Naturally, cats and humans have been living together for longer than that but not as closely as they do today.

Up to that point in time, cats had been used purely as working animals in the yards, protecting their owners' pantries from vermin, such as mice. They enjoyed a lot of freedom and were not forced to do anything because they seldom came into the houses. However, since those days, humans discovered that cats could also become pets and this changed a lot of things for them.

Instead of enjoying their territory, which ideally stretched over several kilometres, their life was reduced to a paltry 80 square metres or so. Instead of doing their business where it was most strategically valuable for them, they had to learn to use a litter box. Instead of spending most of their day chasing vermin, they were expected to lie quietly in the corner. They have only had about 150 years to bring about all these changes, which is only a blink of an eye, from an evolutionary standpoint.

Bearing that in mind, do not be surprised to find a little wild inner-predator, as I like to call it, hidden inside your pet. This predator instinct is not always obvious and not always easy to detect, but I can guarantee you that you will also see the predator in your Norwegian Forest Cat at some point.

This does not have to be a bad thing. On the contrary, it ensures that your cat has the self-confidence it needs. Its noble gait and unbelievably proud look let us know how privileged we are to be able to share a room with it. However, its inner-predator ensures that it is not afraid when visitors come. It does not hide under the bed, but instead it rubs itself up against the legs of strangers to leave some of its scent on them. A cat with a well-developed inner-predator feels content inside its territory and knows what its owner expects of it, so he does not feel the necessity to leave its urine mark on the sofa, clothes or favourite rug.

If the owner neglects the needs of the cat's inner-predator, this could lead to one of two possible events: Either the cat will become a total "scaredy-cat" who has forgotten what a magnificent animal it is, or the cat mutates into a pompous show-off, who feels it needs to draw attention to itself, pretending to be more important than it really feels itself to be.

If the first variation happens, it will be difficult to get the cat out from under the bed, wardrobe or wherever its hideout could be. Owners hardly ever see them and when they do, they appear as ghosts, pressed closely to the wall in their home. Visitors would not imagine that there is even a cat in the house, if it were not for an overpowering smell of urine. Scaredy-cats tend not to leave their hiding places, even if they a desperate to relieve themselves. If their owner misguidedly puts the litter box and food under the bed or inside the wardrobe, that poor, sad animal has no more reason to leave its hiding place.

The pompous show-off is the absolute opposite. It makes sure it is not ignored and that everyone knows that it is there. It likes to stand in people's way and often leaves its mark on things, not only urine but scratch marks on the furniture and walls. Inside, the show-off is just as insecure as the scaredy-cat but it shows it in a different, excessive way.

In both cases, the experts recognise that there is an imbalance in the cat's inner-predator which, unfortunately, is not very easy to heal. That is why it is so important that young cats are raised to have a well-developed inner-predator and that owners understand the needs of their pets. (We will be going deeper into that subject in the chapter called "Your kitten's Basic Needs".)

I see all too often, that people regard their cats as possessions. Perhaps you are thinking that it is not the case with you, but I will explain exactly what I mean, using this example:

Imagine that you come home completely exhausted after a tiring day at work. Suddenly, the telephone rings and the police are at the other end. They tell you that your husband or wife – the soul of a person – has been involved in a fight and that he or she can now be collected from the police station.

What is your first thought in this situation? Most probably it would be something like this: "How could this happen and what can I do to help my husband/wife?" You would like to know what has happened because you know that this is not typical behaviour for your partner. You know that he/she is not violent by nature. You may also wonder how you can support him/her in this difficult situation and what you can do to avoid this happening again.

Now imagine that, instead of the telephone ringing, you see that your little Norwegian Forest Cat has relieved itself on both your new couch and the rug while you were out.

What are your first thoughts? Most probably they would be something like this: "Why is it doing this to me and how am I going to get the stains out?" Unlike the situation with your partner, your thoughts are not about the “why” and “how can I help” but probably about your damaged possessions and you will think of a way to solve the mess. I have to admit that it was the same for me. Until I learned that I should not see my cat as my “possession” but as a companion which has its own needs and with whom I share a home. It is essential for the good development of the inner-predator in your Norwegian Forest kitten to see things from this point of view. You should always treat your cat as a companion as you would if it were a human. See everything you do as if your cat were another person. If it is only another possession for you, I can already prophesy that the inner-predator in it would waste away, which would not be good for either of you. You will read all about what to do when the inner-predator appears and how you should deal with it in the following chapters.

Special Characteristics of your Norwegian Forest Cat

You can recognise the inner-predator of your Norwegian Forest Cat best by looking at its play instinct and desire to climb. When you watch your kitten play, the many parallels to its wild cousins are very noticeable.

It is important for you to know that hunting is not just a pastime or hobby for your Norwegian Forest Cat, which it can cultivate, but it is absolutely essential for it. Hunting is an essential part of its life and you must not only accept that but ideally also support and reinforce its instinctive behaviour with ritualised games. So, you need to know right from the beginning that you will have to participate in simulated hunting games with your Norwegian Forest Cat – this is as obligatory as taking a dog out for a walk.

And I can promise you: It can be fun. Watching your cat hunt, how it behaves, what tactic it uses is not only entertaining but is a great way to help you to bond to become real partners.

THE MAGIC SPELL

People often ask me if there is a trick or a magic spell to turn every kitten into a well-behaved cat. Disregarding for a moment what I think about people who always try to find the simplest way to reach their goals, there is in reality a kind of magic spell, but this looks very different from what people are expecting. My magic spell on what you need to do to be successful in raising a well-behaved cat is – as simply as it sounds – made of only three components:

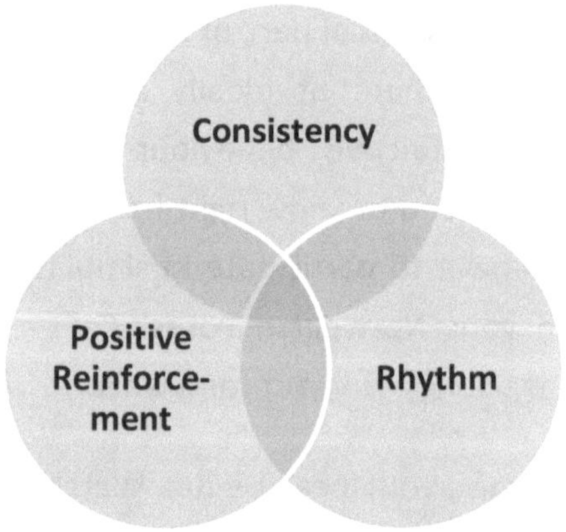

Perhaps you are now thinking: "Is that all? So simple?"

From experience I can tell you: Do not underestimate these three components. You have to cultivate all three of them. If you are consistent but do not give positive reinforcement, you will not be as successful as you want to be. If you are not consistent (or much more frequently others living in your household) you can try as hard as you like with positive reinforcement and rhythm, but your cat will probably be badly-behaved all its life. You will only be successful in raising your Norwegian Forest Cat to be well-behaved when you get all three components working together. By successful I mean effective. As you know, some people reach their goals much quicker than others. That is not usually just a question of luck but because they do something a little different from the others. You will also be one of those successful people if you stick to the three rules: Positive reinforcement, consistency and rhythm.

Let us have a closer look at these three components, starting with the positive reinforcement.

Many cat owners underestimate their cats, not knowing that they are as sensitive as dogs. Their self-confidence and independence give the impression that they do not care much about their owners and are not as receptive as dogs. This is wrong. Cats are very sensitive animals and they are able to build very strong relationships with people. They are also able to recognise changes in mood and know if we are satisfied with certain conduct or not.

It is true that most cats strongly resist anything which has to do with pressure, force or stress. This behaviour is even more prominent in young cats, as in your case. This is why positive reinforcement is so important in raising cats. Your Norwegian Forest Cat will not accept being made to behave in a certain way, using force. This is not a suitable way to train any animal, particularly if you want to live together with them in the long-term. As with most animals, the way to a cat's heart is through its stomach.

This is my tip: Use positive reinforcement, in the form of treats, to signal to your Norwegian Forest Cat when it has done something right. Always treat it immediately (timing is an essential factor here) when it has done something exactly as you want it. This way you will help your Norwegian Forest Cat to understand what is right and what is wrong. That alone will not always make it behave as you wish when you wish it. Often, as I previously mentioned, cats do not see the point in always making their owner happy with their behaviour. However, if you use positive reinforcement from the beginning, in the form of treats or petting time, it ensures that your Norwegian Forest Cat will see a reason to behave in such a way when it profits from its actions.

The next component is consistency. It sounds as if it would be very easy to be consistent when raising your cat, but the reality looks very different. If, for example, you have decided that the dining table is taboo for your Norwegian Forest Cat, you have to forbid it to go on there all the time

– I mean ALWAYS. As soon as you start to make exceptions, perhaps because you are exhausted from work and cannot be bothered to get up from your comfortable couch and tell it for the third time to get down from the dining table. This can have disastrous consequences on everything which your cat has learned up to that point.

Unlike us, your cat is not able to distinguish between everyday occurrences and exceptions. If you allow it (or tolerate it more like) to behave in that way, you will confuse your Norwegian Forest Cat. This confusion will lead to it to believe that the dining room table is not always taboo and it will often put it to the test to see what it can get away with. The consequence of that is that your cat will question any other taboo behaviour which you have set in the past.

My tip for you: When you decide on something, ALWAYS stick to it EVERYWHERE. Excuses and exceptions should not be allowed – I am really firm about that. With a single exception you can ruin the work of weeks! Always remember that it is not enough for only you to be consistent, all the people in your household and all visitors must do the same. Your Norwegian Forest Cat may not be allowed to do something forbidden by one of these people. Being consistent sounds so easy but, in my eyes, it is the most difficult of the three components, as it applies to every day and every night, whether you feel like it or not.

Now we have arrived at our third and last component – the rhythm. Very few cat owners take notice of this component and you can see that on their cats immediately. I personally describe cats as energy vacuums as they are able to quickly suck up all the energy around them. Our job as owners is to find a vent for this energy so that they do not explode – usually causing unwanted behaviour – and to do this, a good rhythm makes all the difference. In most households the energy levels start to rise after getting up in the morning. During this time, your cat will be particularly active and should not be neglected by you. As well as feeding you should, for example, always plan in a game with it to open the valve for its stored energy. The next energy boost will happen at the latest when you come home from work. I recommend playing a little with it then too. The final energy boost of the day will probably come when you are getting ready to go to bed. If you want to avoid your cat's energy from erupting at night, you will probably need to play another round with it.

It is not easy to find the right rhythm but it is worth it. Your cat will always charge its batteries when there is a lot going on. That is because of its inner predator in it, which is trained to switch to hunting mode when there is a lot going on around it. In the early days, it was exactly then that the cat was able to find its prey, hunt it and eat it. You will not be able to get this rhythm out of it but you can adjust to its needs and play a hunting game with it as an alternative. If you keep to this plan faithfully, you will see that your Norwegian Forest Cat does not get up to mischief as much as other cats whose inner-predator is not understood.

THE BIGGEST MISTAKES

One of the biggest mistakes made when raising cats - the assumption that cats cannot be trained - has already been discussed here. Unfortunately, there are many other mistakes which people make and continue to persist in making. Below, you can see the most common of them and I will give you my opinion about them.

Mistake Number 1: Cats are devious and unpredictable.

I have often heard that cats are devious compared to dogs. Firstly, they enjoy being stroked by us and then they will suddenly lash out or bite us. Nearly everyone knows these stories, but the truth is that cats warn us several times before they resort to fighting. Most people are not able to understand the signs. If the cat begins whipping its tail, twitch its skin muscles, pulls its ears back or turns its eyes away, these are clear signals that the cat does not want to be stroked anymore. Every other cat would understand these signals and stop. Once the human has learned to understand the cat language, he will realise that cats are by no means devious and unpredictable.

Mistake Number 2: Cats are always loners

It is true that some wild cats live as loners but this cannot be transferred one-to-one with today's pet cats. Cats, like people, are individuals, and some value company more than others, so it is important not to discount the possibility that your cat could be interested in having a partner. In fact, I have often noticed that two cats flourish more together than when they are kept alone. I would recommend to those who are interested to adopt two kittens at the same time. Relationships with humans cannot compare with those with their own kind. It is important to think carefully before bringing two cats together which do not know each other and to make sure that you take your time in getting them used to each other. It could take several months before cats confront each other for the first time in your home.

Mistake Number 3: Cats and dogs are like fire and ice

Who has not heard the assumption that dogs and cats cannot get along together? Many think that there are two types of people: Cat people and dog people. You probably saw it in various cartoon films when you were young where cats and dogs cannot live together. Of course, this is absolute nonsense. Naturally, there are exceptions but if they are introduced to each other correctly, they can get along very well together, particularly if this takes place when they are very young. At the beginning they could misunderstand each other's body language as there are not many similarities between them, but they are both able to learn each other's language, so there is nothing to stop them from living together. I personally am a big fan of that.

Mistake Number 4: My cat urinates outside the litter box out of spite.

I can tell you categorically that cats do not know spite. We humans tend to project our own behavioural patterns onto our cats. If your Norwegian Forest Cat often refuses to use the litter box, there is another cause. First and foremost, you should ask a vet to exclude any health conditions which could be causing it. Once that has been established, you can look around for other reasons why this is happening. Perhaps it is an enclosed litter box, which many cats do not like. Perhaps the litter box is not clean enough, is standing in the wrong place or your cat links it with some negative experience. It could also be caused by boredom or stress, and there is a possibility that it may refuse to use the litter box if your cat's inner-predator is not developed properly. We will be going into this subject further in the chapter called "House Training".

Mistake number 5: The human is only a tin-opener.

You often hear from so-called cat-haters that cats only see their owners as tin-openers. But this is wrong. Cats can build very close relationships with their humans. However, they are not able to (or better - their inner-predator will not allow them to) show their affection as openly as a pet dog would, for example. But in their own way, cats can show clearly how much they are attached to their humans.

Mistake Number 6: A purring cat is always content.

This is another mistake which will not go away. Of course, cats purr when they are content – but not only then. Cats also purr if they are excited and are probably trying to calm themselves. Scientists have even speculated that the purring of the cat activates its self-healing powers.

Mistake Number 7: Cats do not mind being alone.

It is true that cats are well able to be alone, but they can also get bored. If a person does not ensure that his cat has enough things to occupy it, he can be sure that his cat will get bored at home. If this goes on for too long, it will probably lead to behavioural problems. This is the reason why I like the idea of having two cats, although this is not absolutely necessary. If you are able to occupy your cat sufficiently when you are there and take on board the tips for making your home suitable for cats (particularly with such things as the cat cinema), you can prevent your cat from becoming bored.

You have noticed that there is much prejudice towards cats and some of that is due to incorrect knowledge within society which has firmly taken root. Do not be discouraged. Instead, you can show them, with your Norwegian Forest Cat, that they are wrong about their prejudices.

THE KITTEN'S BASIC NEEDS

As you already know, there is a real predator hidden inside your little kitten, and this predator defines your kitten's basic needs. In principle, these are explained quickly and are easy to remember, as they are the following:

hunting – capturing – killing – eating – resting

Every cat – and I mean EVERY cat – needs these components in its life to be happy. Remember that kittens like yours have only been living in human homes for about 150 years. Up to then, cats were used almost everywhere as working animals, keeping mice and other vermin away from the pantries of the day (i.e., hunting – capturing – killing – eating – resting).

People often ask if it is really necessary for them to play with their Norwegian Forest Cat every day or if it is ok to leave them on their own for a few days, if there is enough food left for them. At the beginning, I tried to answer this question in detail but, in the meantime, I have given up trying. Anyone who is seriously thinking of doing that should not be thinking of getting a cat and is not talking to the right person.

The average wild Norwegian Forest Cat spends at least 15% of its day hunting. It makes about 20 to 30 attempts at catching its prey and is successful in about a third of them. It needs 8 mice a day to cover its calorie needs. Now think of your kitten: Can you really believe that it is enough for it to be given its food and to do without the enjoyment of the hunt? Miss the excitement of catching something (and playing with it)?

Cats are hunters. They love hunting and only a day when they can hunt – capture – kill – eat – rest is a truly fulfilling day for them. Remember that and make sure that you give your cat (and its inner-predator) what it needs. It is best to play with your cat for a while before feeding it, but we will get to that later.

Unfortunately, I keep hearing that there are cats which do not want to play. Here I can only say: Cats always want to play. The reason for this false reasoning is often easy to see. Either the cat owners have not understood how their cat likes to play yet or they falsely believe that playing means that the cat must run around the home non-stop for an hour.

It is not only the active hunting game (i.e., springing onto its prey) which is considered playing by your cat but it also loves to creep up and watch its prey. For some cats that is more important than the actual catch. Find out what your cat likes doing best.

In case you are asking what the cat does for the rest of the day I can give you one answer. At least half the day is spent preening and a further 20% looking out of the window (I will explain later how you can make this the absolute highlight of the day).

Special Characteristics of your Norwegian Forest Cat

The Norwegian Forest Cat breed is very playful, so you will probably not have a problem finding out which games your kitten loves best.

At the same time, you have an even greater responsibility. Since the official beginning of its breeding, great importance has been attached to enhancing its play and climbing instinct. You should be aware that encouraging the play instinct of your Norwegian Forest Cat is extremely important. A single round of play per day is definitely not enough for this breed to have a happy life. You must be ready to integrate several playtimes into your daily routine, right from the start.

Doing that will not only keep your cat happy, but it will also increase the bond between you both. You will feel it ... and love it!

- Chapter 3 -

Before Your Young Cat Arrives

The preparation for raising your cat begins long before your little Norwegian Forest Cat moves in. One part of that is reading this handbook thoroughly, preferably a few times. By all means make “dog-ears” on the most important pages. This book is meant to be worked with and not put on the shelf, unused.

After that, you will need to make a few decisions and preparations for your future relationship with your kitten. You will notice that some things will change in your homelife once your new housemate moves in.

You will want to know exactly what to expect, so we will be speaking about the following subjects on the pages to come:

- **The primary human:** Who is suitable to be the main caregiver for the kitten?
- **The privileges:** Decide in advance what you will allow your cat to do and what is absolutely taboo.

- **The time factor:** Do not underestimate how much of your time a kitten, but also how much time a fully-grown cat will need.
- **The home:** Make sure that your home is suitable for a cat living there before it arrives.

If you have considered these five points, you are well prepared to receive your newcomer! Later on in this book under the title "Checklist for the Start", you will see a detailed checklist which will summarise what you should consider and what you will need.

THE PRIMARY HUMAN

The first decision which has to be made is who will take care of the little one. This is a very challenging and time-consuming responsibility. For this reason, it cannot be left to a child. Even if it is well-meant, it will not be a good choice for your Norwegian Forest Cat. Kittens think of children as companions and play friends but not as examples on which they can orientate themselves.

The job of the primary human is not only to take over the main responsibilities of raising the cat, but to play a mainly sovereign and authoritative role. The primary human of a kitten is responsible for recognising danger early and making sure that the rules of the house are kept consistently and at the same time showing self-confidence. This person is also responsible for feeding and ensures the general health and happiness of the cat.

If children live in your household, it is essential that they play their part in raising the kitten. I think it is wonderful when children learn very early to take responsibility for feeding and keeping animal. But please ensure that your child is not over-stressed and is able to enjoy the experience. A child's first experience with animals will impact its whole life. Encouraging your child to help you to look after your cat will not only make the cat happy but could also produce a future cat fan.

It is also important that you, as the primary human, constantly ask yourself if you are doing everything correctly with regards to your Norwegian Forest Cat. As with all things, carelessness can creep up on you. You should also never forget to ask yourself if you are treating your Norwegian Forest Cat as a possession or as a living, sentient being.

Special Characteristics of your Norwegian Forest Cat

It is important to nominate a primary human while raising any cat. However, you do not need to worry that it will be so fixated on you and ignore every other member of your family. Its sociable and friendly nature will ensure that all members of the household (including other animals) will become part of its close circle.

THE PRIVILEGES

Once the primary human has been chosen, the next step is to set privileges. You will need to decide in advance how you want your relationship with your Norwegian Forest Cat to be. This includes what you allow and what you do not allow.

I suggest you make the decision before you are enchanted by those big, sweet cat eyes. Decide precisely what you want. As an example, I am not a fan of letting cats sleep on my bed and I do not want them on the kitchen tops or dining room table. The pantry is taboo and so is the sewing room. Apart from those places, my kitty is allowed to go anywhere it wants.

These were my examples, yours could be completely different. For example, there is nothing against letting your cat sleep on your bed, I just do not like it, particularly since I once inadvertently turned over onto my sweet kitty in the night and woke up scratched and bitten. The other places I mention are out of bounds for hygiene reasons.

It is important when forbidding a cat to do something that you offer an alternative. I will go into that in further detail in the subsection called "How to Praise and Berate Correctly". This is very important if there are parts of the kitchen which they are not allowed to go on, such as the kitchen sideboard. For my cat, it does not make sense that I do not want her there, precisely because there are always exciting and good-smelling things going on there which she naturally wants to explore and observe.

Your Norwegian Forest Cat will not accept simply being shut out of such places, so it is always good to offer it an alternative. In my case, I placed a cat tree next to the kitchen sideboard, so that it can see everything that is going on in the kitchen and my kitty is happy with the compromise.

When you intend to forbid something, you must always think of a way to offer an alternative.

Special Characteristics of your Norwegian Forest Cat

Your Norwegian Forest Cat will grow to a length of 130 cm and weigh 9.5 kg, making it a very large cat. In addition, it has a semi-long, dense fur which will moult a great deal.

I suggest you think very carefully which privileges you allow your kitten. Always remember that it will not remain as small as it is at that moment but will grow into a comparatively large and heavy house cat.

At first, having your kitten in bed with you is probably still sweet, but at some point, it will take up a lot of space. It is always easier to teach a kitten, from the start, that there are rooms which it is not allowed to go into, than it is to teach a fully-grown cat that a room, which it has regarded up to now as a part of its territory, is no longer allowed. Banning an adult cat from the bed is even more difficult.

THE TIME FACTOR

Thirdly, you must decide how much time you are willing to invest in your new companion. Most cat owners underestimate how much time it takes to raise their cats properly and inadvertently set the stage for their Norwegian Forest Cats to develop behavioural abnormalities.

To ensure that does not happen to you, you need to be clear how much time you will need – and you will need a lot. Your little Norwegian Forest Cat will not want to be alone for a long time during the first weeks and months. In addition, someone must diligently keep an eye on what it is doing, so that it does not develop any bad behavioural patterns.

The first few weeks are among the most important for your lives together, so you should muster as much time as you can for your little kitty. If you are working, take a few weeks' holiday. The old saying "You cannot teach an old dog new tricks" goes for cats too. Everything which you fail to teach them in the first few weeks and months will become more difficult to teach them when they are older.

Of course, the time you need to spend will reduce after basic education is complete, your Norwegian Forest Cat becomes an adult, and you have found your daily rhythm with each other, but you need to know that it will never stop altogether. A cat is not a loner, it will always need your attention and time, no matter how old it is. You will need to occupy it every day and, just like dog owners have to take their dogs for walks several times a day, you will need to clean its litter box and play with it several times a day.

I cannot stress enough that most behavioural disorders are caused by the owners spending too little time with their cats, or giving them the wrong kind of attention. As your Norwegian Forest Cat is not a possession, which has to comply, but a dependent with whom you like to spend time, this should not be a problem for you.

Special Characteristics of your Norwegian Forest Cat

You are very lucky with your Norwegian Forest Cat because it is much more receptive to your control than other breeds because of its open and friendly character. For that reason, the settling-in phase could be much quicker.

Unfortunately, because of the above, many people's expectations of their cats become too great and they very quickly become discontented and frustrated. Always remember that your Norwegian Forest Cat has only been a domesticated animal for about 150 years. Apart from that, every individual within the breed is different and should not be lumped together. It is possible that one Norwegian Forest Cat learns quicker or adapts better than another. We, as humans and owners, should be aware of that and make allowances.

I suggest that, if at all possible, your Norwegian Forest kitten should be given a few weeks grace to settle in

The Home

Now we come to the great subject of preparing your home. It never ceases to amaze me how many cat owners make no effort at all to prepare their homes for their new companion. Either they are unwilling to do it or they do not have enough knowledge and are ignorant of their kitten's needs, which is far more common.

To ensure that this does not happen to you, we will go through the necessary preparations to make a cat-friendly home over the next few pages. There are basically four main factors.

- The litter box
- The cat tree
- The cat playground/catwalk
- The cat cinema

Let us start with the **litter box**, as it is the thing which most cat owners dread. After all, who wants to have a litter box in the middle of the living room and watch their cat doing its business?

Honestly: I am not a great fan of them either. However, my long experience tells me that there is no real alternative to it. Of course, I have heard stories about cats which have been trained to use the human toilet. Perhaps there are a few individuals who find it alright, but most cats would not be happy doing that. Remember what you have learned about the inner-predator inside your Norwegian Forest Cat and how important it is for them to mark their territory with their scents. The litter box goes a long way towards satisfying that need.

After accepting that the litter box is unavoidable, the question arises about how many of them are necessary. My general answer is: Always at least one more litter box than there are cats in the household. Therefore, with one cat you will needs at least two litter boxes and with two cats at least three, and so on.

Why is one litter box not enough? Most cats like to use different litter boxes for their small and big businesses. I recommend offering these two alternatives to avoid your cat from choosing its own places, such as the plant pot or wardrobe. Cats have no problem sharing their litter boxes, you will not need to buy two litter boxes every time you take on a new cat. That said, you can never have too many litter boxes.

Now we come to the next important question: Where to put the litter box. Where you have a problem cat, who pees in the house, it is often the case that a litter box is put in a way-off place, such as the bathroom, the hall, or even the cellar or garage. These often remain untouched in their places.

Ask yourself if these places are suitable, now that you know about the inner-predator and the needs of your Norwegian Forest Cat. The answer is no!

Cats do their businesses exactly where they find the most energy in the home. That usually means the rooms which you usually frequent. Even though it may not seem nice to do so, you will need to put litter boxes exactly in those places. In my case it is the living room, kitchen and bedroom. It is really important that you do not consider the aesthetic aspect of this, but instead think of the needs of your Norwegian Forest Cat.

Please do not put a litter box in a secluded corner of the room or even put flowers around it so that you do not have to look at it. Cats prefer to be able to see everything when they are doing their businesses. For this reason, I recommend using open litter boxes only. If yours has a lid, please take it off. You will know that cats do not like to be cornered. They scan the area, looking for possible ways of escape. A cat could find itself feeling trapped in a corner and stop using the litter box altogether. Try to find an open place for it, which allows an entrance and exit in more than one direction.

Remember the size of your cat, when buying a litter box. Your Norwegian Forest Cat is a big specimen, and your litter box should correspond to that. Your cat should be able to turn around in it when it is fully grown. The entrance should be placed so that a kitten can enter and leave without problems. If even the smallest obstacle is in its way, you may find that your cat will not use the litter box.

There are differing opinions about what to fill your litter box with. At the beginning, I would recommend using a litter which your cat has been used to at the breeder or animal shelter. Ask for the brand name and use the identical one. You can stay with that one or try to find out carefully what your cat likes. Here I can only stress that it is a trial-and-error process. Try different degrees of softness and size. My experience has been that cats normally prefer a softer litter.

You will learn how to teach your cat to use the cat litter in the chapter called “House Training”.

This brings us to the **cat tree**. I am often asked if it is at all necessary as it could destroy the aestheticism of any room. The answer to that is very simple: If you do not want your cat to scratch your furniture and walls, you cannot avoid getting a cat tree. In reality one cat tree will not be enough. There should be one in every room in which the cat spends any length of time.

It is important that you understand that cats do not scratch for fun and certainly not out of spite or to upset you. Cats scratch to stretch their chest or back muscles. In addition, they reduce stress in this way and at the same time remove the outside layer of their claws. However, much more importantly, these scratches represent the territorial rights of your cat. Scratching gives your cat the feeling of security and ownership. Just like we put pictures on the wall, which we sometimes straighten, cats adjust their scratches when they pass by them.

In addition, your cat is mixing its own scent with yours when scratching. For this reason, cats would not choose to scratch an unpopular corner of the sofa which no one would see, but would prefer exactly your favourite place as this smells of you and is the most interesting for them.

There are all types of cat tree, varying in size and materials. Most importantly, it must be stable. If it wobbles when used, or is jumped on enthusiastically, your cat will not like to use it. It should also be suitably-sized for your room tiger, which means for your Norwegian Forest Cat that you will need to get a larger version. It is important that there is enough space for it to be able to stretch out and must have a large enough scratch area.

If you are wondering where to put the cat tree, I would suggest putting it in the place which is most interesting for your Norwegian Forest Cat. It could be, for example next to the couch, at the window, next to the kitchen tops or at your writing desk. It should be placed where you are most often to be found and where your scent is very present. If your cat does not use the cat tree and instead prefers the sofa, you will learn how to deal with that in the next chapter "Destructive Behaviour".

While most people have heard of cat trees and litter boxes, few people know what a "**catwalk**" is, although it is very important.

As you already know, cats perceive rooms not only horizontally but also vertically, and are used to using them that way. For most cats it is a matter of fact not only to move around on the floor, but also to use cupboards, tables and shelves. If you do not like them doing this, or if they inadvertently knock down books - or worse, vases and pictures – due to lack of space, then you need to offer them an alternative.

By far the best alternative is the so-called catwalk. Here you would plan a concept how your cat can move along on various levels in a room without touching the floor.

Think of a series of walkways which your cat can use and put your plan into action. The best method for making the walkways is to use planks which you can fix to the walls. Please make sure that they are fixed firmly and wide enough that two cats can pass each other on them.

Try to find interesting ways for your cat to walk to, where it has a good view over the room. Place rest areas in strategic places, such as a comfortable basket or a hammock. Use your imagination.

Never forget to plan sufficient entries and exits into your design. As previously mentioned, your Norwegian Forest Cat is always looking for ways to escape if necessary. Cat trees can be useful as exits as well as steps or ladders.

Once you have well-planned catwalk in all your important rooms, the inner-predator of your Norwegian Forest Cat will be very happy. You will see that your cat becomes much more self-confident as it can take part in family affairs (from a safe distance) and see everything that is going on. It can move around freely as the catwalk is its own personal territory which is not used by anyone else. It is your cat's refuge and you will see that your shelves, fridges and tables will be much less frequented. The catwalk is worth its weight in gold, particularly if you have children or often have visitors. Your Norwegian Forest Cat will always have a place to retreat to, but still has the possibility to participate in social life, if it wishes.

I would like to give you one last tip regarding the catwalk: Make your design so that you are always able to get your cat down if you need to, without too much effort.

On the following page, you can see an example of how to arrange your living room so it is suitable for the cat's needs. Below you will see how many cat owners unfortunately prefer to have their rooms, followed by an example of how to cater to your cat's needs.

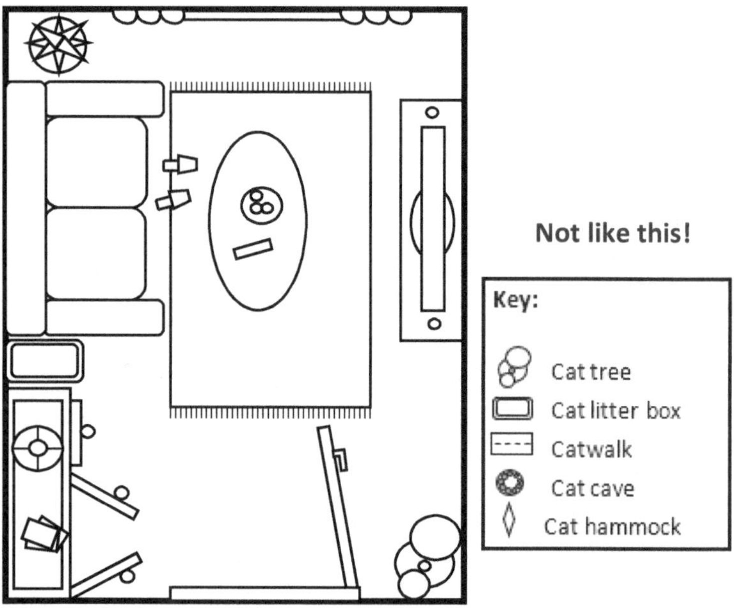

It is important to note that the catwalk is built at varying heights (and, if you wish, with varying materials), even though this is not apparent from the diagram.

This is much better!

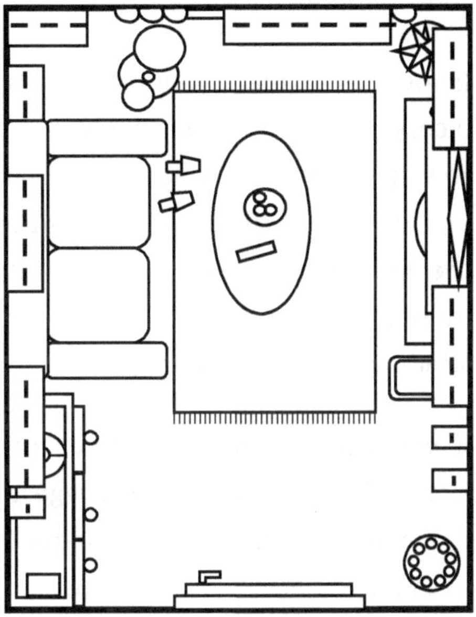

Key:

Cat tree
Cat litter box
Catwalk
Cat cave
Cat hammock

You will probably have noticed that, in the second diagram, I have moved the cat tree from behind the door to the window. This has two distinct advantages: Firstly, your cat is close to you when you are sitting on the sofa, and secondly, it is in the best spot for the well-loved **cat cinema.**

By cat cinema I do not mean that your cat spends its time watching a series of films. It is much more interesting for your cat to see what is happening on the other side of the window. Cats are hunters and as such are used to observing quietly over long periods of time, and to this day it is one of their favourite hobbies.

If you want to make your cat very happy, you should find it a cosy place for it to watch what is going on. Most cats like to watch out of the window and that is not without reason and where they sit changes with the sun's movement during the day. My cats like to sit at east-facing windows during the mornings and change to south-facing and later west-facing windows as the day goes on.

If you want to make it particularly interesting for your Norwegian Forest Cat, I suggest providing a lot of movement in front of the window. You can do this, for example, by placing a bird house or bird bath outside the window. An insect hotel is interesting for them too. Use your imagination and try various ideas out as to how you can provide your cat with some variety. An aquarium is very interesting for cats too. However, I would not recommend buying one specifically to use as a cat cinema. If you already have one, make sure that it is securely closed and safe from your cat being able to open it.

Now that we have discussed the cat litter box, the cat tree, the catwalk and the cat cinema, I have three further tips for you:

1. **Do not allow your Norwegian Forest kitten freedom to go everywhere in your home at first, this will overtax the little creature.** I suggest to establish a so-called base camp in any room which you choose. This should be a room where you too spend much of your time. The room should be prepared with all the things which you have learned about in the previous pages, including toys. It is always a good idea to place something in the room which smells of its old home, in order to make the changeover as easy as possible. If you got your cat from a breeder, you could have the possibility of bringing it a toy or basket at least a week before you pick it up so that it will take on the scent of your cat's siblings and parents. This will give your little kitten the feeling that everything is not completely strange to it. If you got your kitten from an animal shelter, or you might not had time to bring it something to the breeder, you should see if there is anything, no matter how small, that you can bring with your kitten when it comes to live with you.

   As soon as you notice that your kitten is slowly getting used to her room, you can get her used to the next rooms step by step. You can tell by the fact that she moves confidently thorough the room that she is ready, especially if she has sniffed and inquired everything. Do not be impatient, it could take several days with a shy cat until it starts to feel comfortable in its new home. Do not show it all the rooms from the beginning, just one at a time. Once it has got used to one room you can show it the next. This will slowly but surely increase the size of your little cat's universe. To ease the move into a new room, I suggest that you take something from the old room with you and place it in the new room. This could perhaps be the cat tree from the base camp which you take into the new room and move the cat tree from the new room back into the base camp.

2. **Cats are like small children, so you should make your home "child safe" before the kitten arrives.** What do I mean with that? Put everything which is breakable or things which you treasure out of its reach. By "out of its reach" I mean locking things away into cupboards or moving them into rooms where your cat is not allowed. Remember

that, unlike children, a cat's world is vertical as well as horizontal. You should also check if there are any cables lying around which could be dangerous for your kitten. If your cat is very talented at opening cupboards – which is very possible with your Norwegian Forest Cat – I suggest applying child-proof locks to the doors. I would also lock away any expensive rugs or furniture at the beginning. When your cat is house-trained, has settled in and you think it is "safe", you could consider slowly putting your things back in place, one by one. Moreover, you will need to find out which plants are poisonous for your Norwegian Forest Cat and ban them from your home.

3. **Keep questioning your room concept.** If this is your first cat, I recommend looking carefully how your cat is reacting to your room concept. Does it seem to like it or are there corners that she hardly uses? If so, why? Be watchful and offer alternatives for things which do not work as well as you originally expected them to. Of course, it makes sense to swap things around to offer some variety, but this does not mean that you should change your home around

every week. It could mean changing a cat tree occasionally or adding a hammock. You could also consider occasionally changing something about your cat cinema.

Special Characteristics of your Norwegian Forest Cat

The size and weight of your fully-grown Norwegian Forest Cat should play an important role in everything you plan in your home. You need to think a size larger than many other cat-owners.

Get some detailed advice from a pet shop about the size of the litter box or cat bed to make sure it will be the right size. If you are getting your kitten from a breeder, this person will usually give you valuable tips about the size your kitten will grow to.

In my opinion, Norwegian Forest Cats are not very suitable to be kept purely inside the home as they are very active and need a lot of activity. As they are intelligent and very playful, I suggest thinking hard about the design of your cat cinema. A well-designed cat cinema is a fairly good alternative to the garden. Your cat will love seeing what is going on outside.

You will also need to design a very well-devised catwalk for your Norwegian Forest Cat with a lot of opportunities for your cat to make jumps. You can use a variety of materials and surfaces rather than plain wooden planks. You could offer your cat an interesting suspension bridge for example. Use your imagination.

You will probably need a large number of toys and will need to swap them over regularly, in contrast to owners of a less playful breed. Your Norwegian Forest Cat will want a lot of variety and alternatives, and this also includes its cat tree.

If you live in a very small home and perhaps also share it with others, this could be made a lot worse by having a Norwegian Forest Cat. In smaller homes, the higher areas are often used for storage which will make it more difficult to integrate a catwalk into your planning and possibly there will not be room for cat trees, etc. Make sure in advance that there is enough room for you and your Norwegian Forest Cat and all its needs. It would be a shame if lack of space leads to unnecessary problems which can often lead to the cat being taken to the animal shelter.

- Chapter 4 -

THE FIRST WEEKS

At last! Your Norwegian Forest Cat is moving in with you. It should be at least 10 weeks old by now, even better 12 weeks. If a breeder offers you a younger kitten, you should stay clear of him as he is probably not a reputable breeder.

It is very important for a Norwegian Forest Cat to be with its mother and siblings during the first weeks. In this time, it learns a lot about social behaviour and begins to imitate its mother. The longer a kitten is with its mother, the better it is for its future.

At some point the time is right for the kitten to leave its familiar world and move in with you. To avoid this ending in drama read on and I will tell you about:

- How to help your kitten settle in,
- How to bond with it from an early date,
- How to praise and berate it correctly,
- How to train it to be alone and
- How to understand the body language of your kitten.

HOW TO SETTLE IN YOUR KITTEN

Before your Norwegian Forest Cat moves in with you, it must make the transition between the breeder or animal shelter and your home. This alone is a big adventure for your little cat. You should try to make the journey as pleasant as possible, after all, you will want to start your relationship off in a positive way so that it does not experience its first trauma.

If your kitten knows and accepts the transport box, you can use this. If, however, it has not yet experienced the transport box, I have found it better not to use one for this journey. Instead, it is better to take your kitten in your arms. If you are travelling in the car, it would be helpful for another person to take over the driving for you, so that you can look after your kitten without stress.

When you arrive, it is important that everything goes calmly. Take your transport box (or kitten) directly into its base camp and put it down in the corner. Close by, put down the blanket or toy which you have brought with you from the breeder or animal shelter so that the little one has a familiar smell near it in this strange new place. At this point there should be no one else in the room and certainly no other animals. Close the door and open the transport box, putting it a little distance from you on the floor, then wait.

Your cat will determine the pace of its settling in and not you.

Some cats will come bolting out of the box straight away and bravely take in its new surroundings, perhaps even playing with you. However, that is not always the case. Shy animals often stay in their box for a longer period of time, perhaps until you have left the room – some even wait until night time.

This is not the behaviour that most new cat owners would like but it is normal. It is better to be prepared that your kitten may be hesitant and then you will not be disappointed.

What you must definitely not do is to take your kitten straight out of its transport box. The kitten must decide to look around its new surroundings by itself. If you take it out against its will, your kitten will make negative associations with both you and the base camp. Be patient and allow your kitten to decide when it is ready.

I suggest that, for the first day – and preferably the first week – you do not receive any visitors. Of course, I know how proud you are of your new family member and you would like to present it to everyone straight away. But please remember that everything is new for your Norwegian Forest Cat and that it has lost all its familiar environment, including other animals and humans, all at once. Do not overstress or confuse it by exposing it to too many new faces. It is particularly important that you and your kitten build up a bond in the first few days. The more people it meets, the more difficult it will be to build and strengthen the bond with you.

Stay in the base camp as much as you can during the first few days. Sit on the floor (then you do not look so big and threatening) and wait to see how your kitten reacts. Is it curious and comes straight towards you? Or is it a little reluctant and prefers to watch you from a distance?

If it is the former, you can begin playing a few hunting games with it, for example with a play fishing rod. This has the advantage that it can keep its distance from you – your kitten does not have to be too close to you to play. During play, you will awaken the inner predator in it and your kitten will begin to concentrate on the hunt, forgetting its fears of you and its new environment. At the same time, it is experiencing something positive. If your cat is ready for that, you can start planning short play times into its day straight away.

If your young cat is a little reluctant, it can help to read it something. It really does not matter what you read (whether it is an exciting novel or the local newspaper). The aim is for your Norwegian Forest Cat to get used to your voice and begin to understand that you are not a danger to it. In addition, your cat will not feel under pressure or watched (after all, you are concentrating on your book or newspaper), but on the contrary can watch you unhindered. With a little patience even reluctant cats will eventually become curious at some point and come towards you.

During the first few days, your cat will spend a lot of time exploring its new environment. It will look in every corner and climb on everything which it can, squeezing itself into every crack. You will be surprised what it can fit into and what it can reach.

I recommend barricading all difficult-to-reach places, such as under the bed or sofa) from the beginning and to keep them barricaded. Do not let your Norwegian Forest Cat get used to going to these places or you will later have to get it out of those habits. If you remember my tip, you will not end up with scratched arms.

Not every settling-in phase runs smoothly. Because of this, I will give you a few tips as to how to cope with the three most common problems:

1. **My cat spends most of its time hiding:**
   This can easily happen. Make life as easy as possible for your kitten. Many reluctant cats are afraid of crossing an open room

because it makes them feel vulnerable. Make hiding places for your cat using cardboard boxes with entries cut into them or put blankets over chairs. This way, you will give your kitten a few "safe" ways to cross the room. Make sure that you have put their food, water and litter box in places where your cat can feel safe and not get stuck in a dead-end without a way to escape. Do not overcrowd your kitten, keep your distance. Your Norwegian Forest Cat must make the first steps towards you. After a few days you can try to awaken its curiosity by throwing a treat towards your cat and waiting. The best time to do this is just before feeding time when your little kitten has an appetite. If it takes the treat, you can throw the next one towards it, so that it has to take a few steps in your direction. Continue to do this and your cat will come nearer and nearer to you. Please do not make the mistake of trying to grab your cat. Instead, offer it the last treat in your hand and keep still. When the time is right, your kitten will take it from you and will be "eating out of your hand" as the saying goes.

2. **My cat will not let me touch it:**

   This can also be a normal reaction to its new environment. As I already mentioned, it is absolutely essential that your kitten makes the first move. Perhaps it will rub itself on your legs or jump onto your lap if you sit on the floor. If your cat does not do that during the first days, there is no need to worry. Just be patient. Spend a lot of time in the base camp, while ideally busying yourself with something else. Many cats do not like it when they feel as if they are being watched. If you take no notice of it, your cat will become curious about you. It can also be useful if you sleep in the base camp. This might make a reluctant cat more fearless. Avoid using strongly perfumed products, and creams and avoid using hand cream altogether at first. Sometimes that is the reason. If your cat is still showing behavioural abnormalities, such as not eating, the cause could be sickness or some kind of pain. If this is the case, it would be better to get it examined straight away by a vet.

3. **My cat will not eat:**

   This is not particularly unusual for the first day, or are you very hungry when you are excited or frightened? I do not think so. If your kitten is otherwise healthy and is drinking, there is nothing to worry about for the time being. Some cats do not eat until it starts to get dark. If it still does not eat the next day, you could try to tempt it with treats. However, if it continues to refuse food for longer than 24 hours, you should consider giving your vet a call.

   You should never change your Norwegian Forest Cat's food directly after moving in. Ask your breeder or shelter to give you a few rations of food with your cat and stay with that, or change it very slowly. Any quick change of diet will lead to diarrhoea, which can quickly become dangerous to such a small creature.

Special Characteristics of your Norwegian Forest Cat

Generally, the Norwegian Forest Cat is considered very playful, sociable and affectionate. In addition, it builds up a very deep and close relationship to its humans. All these things point to the Norwegian Forest Cat normally fitting quickly into its new environment.

Please remember that, despite the general description given here, every kitten is an individual and will display varying characteristics, even if it comes from the same litter.

If your kitten seems very quiet at the breeder, the chances are that this characteristic will get stronger when it moves in with you. However, if your kitten very boldly rushes to greet you at the breeder, there is a greater chance that it will quickly settle into its new environment with you at home.

Finally, we can conclude, that Norwegian Forest kittens will settle in to their new homes quickly (quicker than other breeds) but you need to be aware that there are exceptions to every rule.

HOW TO BUILD A RELATIONSHIP

I already described at the beginning of this book how important the primary human is to your kitten. But how do you become this person? It is not enough just to say that you are. In order to build up a relationship, you will need to spend a lot of time with your little kitten to help it accept, respect and trust you.

At the beginning you will need to give it as many positive experiences as you can which are connected to you. With cats (as with many people) a good way to build up a relationship is to feed it. I suggest that you are the only person who feeds it at the beginning. I do not just mean feeding it and leaving. You need to stay close to it while it is eating, perhaps sitting on the floor near it, reading a book. Do not sit too closely as that could be perceived as threatening. The reason for doing this is that your cat will associate your scent with something positive (the food). This may seem strange at first reading, but it has a very positive effect on your relationship with your cat.

In addition, you need to be the one who plays most with it. Your kitten will learn that everything which is cool, exciting and tasty comes from you and it stores that knowledge subconsciously believing that it can always rely on you.

Once you get the feeling that your Norwegian Forest Cat feels comfortable in its base camp and has taken over its territory confidently, you can begin to make trips with it. Go slowly from one room to the next. Take one room at a time and only expand the territory further when your kitten feels as comfortable in that room as it does in its base camp.

How do you go about exploring the territory?

As you will see in the Chapter "Your Home", you could take out a few of your kitten's marked objects before you begin. For example, you could take the cat tree out of room 2 and swap it with the one in the base camp. You could take a few toys, which your kitten has played with and which have both your scent and your cat's scent on them, and place them in room 2.

Once you have finished with the preparations you can open the door and sit down on the floor in room 2, a little way from the door. Now just wait and watch what your kitty does. As with moving into the new home, it is important that your little cat is the one who makes the decision to explore room 2. Be there for it so that it has the feeling of not being alone but do not do anything. If your cat comes up to you confidently, of course you can pet it or play with it, but do not try to make it enter the new territory. Your kitten will do it by itself when it is ready to do so.

Once this step has been taken, you will enjoy watching your Norwegian Forest Cat exploring the new room. Wait until your kitten feels as comfortable in the new room as in its base camp before you introduce it to the next room in the same way. Some cats take these steps quickly, others take longer. Please go at the speed your kitten feels comfortable with. In my experience, you will need at least two days before introducing each new room. Even if yours is one of the more confident types of cat which has not shown any fear, a new room is a big challenge for it with all the new impressions and information for your kitten to process.

While playing and tumbling with your Norwegian Forest Cat, you should not forget that a baby has entered your home. Babies sleep a lot at the beginning so that they can process all the new impressions and adventures. Even though you need to bond, play and explore with your kitten, you should not forget that it also needs a lot of sleep. Let it sleep and make sure that it is not disturbed.

Special Characteristics of your Norwegian Forest Cat

Due to its ability to form a deep and close bond with its humans, it will not prove very difficult for you to build that relationship with your Norwegian Forest Cat.

It is important that you work hard on this bond and cultivate it. It means spending a lot of time with it so that you can understand its personality as an individual. Find out what it particularly likes to do and which treats it likes best.

You will not regret the time you invest now in your Norwegian Forest Cat. You are building the foundations which will leave a lasting impression on you and you will see how close you become and how well you interact with each other.

Your cat has brought all that is necessary with it. Now it is up to you to do your best. Do not worry, I am sure your Norwegian Forest Cat will not make it difficult for you and instead will be grateful, happy and full of fun.

HOW TO PRAISE AND BERATE CORRECTLY

To praise or berate? Many cat owners ask themselves this question. For me the answer is clear.

Have you ever heard of operant conditioning? This principle can be used throughout the animal world and is based on the assumption that certain events can increase the chances of a certain behaviour repeating itself. In other words, praise can encourage a certain behaviour whereas berating can discourage it.

In my opinion, positive encouragement is the more effective method for generating certain behaviour. Of course, punishment works too – at least in the short term – but it can also cause aggression and fear, both of which are not helpful in building up a trusting foundation with your cat, as described earlier.

You are probably asking yourself – as do many cat owners – how can you discipline your kitten if you cannot berate or punish it? The answer is simple: You cannot, because cats do not allow themselves to be disciplined. This has nothing to do with its quite considerable self-confidence, but on the fact that they cannot establish a connection between the punishment and the crime. They will never understand why they are being berated, which makes the effort a waste of time. In addition, any kind of punishment is bad for its inner-predator, which might become less prominent and that might lead to a loss of your Norwegian Forest Cat's self-confidence and happiness in the future.

This is why I suggest avoiding all forms of berating and punishment. If your cat has urinated on your favourite cushion, remove it quietly and forget about it.

Do not resort to using a spray can to enforce your rules, even though many people swear by it: The proud cat owner only needs to spray once and the cat will jump down from the table. Often it is enough just to pick up the spray can and the cat disappears. Consider what I have previously said about how your cat processes thoughts. Your cat has not learned that it must get off the table, it has learned that when you pick up the spray can, things will get uncomfortable for it. The cat associates you with the source of danger. If it learns to be afraid of you, that is in no way positive. On the contrary, I am convinced that every cat owner who feels that he or she must use fear to assert his/her wishes is doing something fundamentally wrong (this does probably not only apply to cats).

So how do you do it correctly?

People often ask me how to get rid of a certain behaviour. In reality, it is much more important to find out the motivation for the behaviour. I can explain this more clearly using a human example. Let us assume you have a six-year-old son who constantly draws on the walls of your home. Of course, you could continue to forbid him to do that. You could, however, recognise his desire to draw and help him by steering his impulse in a different direction which is better for you. You can do this by buying him an easel and some new crayons. This way you can make him understand that you understand his desire to draw but that he must use the easel instead.

It is much the same with your Norwegian Forest Cat. Get used to not only saying "no" but saying "yes" in the same breath. Always try to recognise the desire behind the so-called bad behaviour and offer an alternative that suits you better.

Let us return the example of the dining room table. Use a "no" which will not connect the rebuke directly with you. For example, you can place a piece of double-sided adhesive tape on the table. If your cat jumps onto this, the result is an unpleasant experience, however, at the same time, the "no" is not directly connected with you).

In order to achieve the following "yes" you must understand the original motivation. It is possible that there may be various factors involved in this case. Your cat is probably interested in the height of the table, because it is able to see everything from there. Secondly, there is often food on the table which is a great attraction for your cat. Thirdly it could be you. You are often sitting at this table and your cat wants to be with you.

Why not put a cat tree close to the dining room table? This should be positioned so that your cat can see everything on the table clearly. You can also encourage it to use the tree by giving it treats (remember the second motivation food). Lastly, I would recommend to put a t-shirt on the tree which you have worn for sport. This will leave a conspicuous scent which your cat will find irresistible.

The earlier and more consistently you use this method of combined "yes" and "no", the better your kitten (and later your adult cat) will understand which behaviour you prefer.

Always try to reward positive behaviour through praise, treats and petting and never punish for bad behaviour. Try to understand the motivation behind it (it is never malice) and offer your cat alternatives for the behaviour.

Special Characteristics of your Norwegian Forest Cat

As I mentioned at the beginning of this handbook, the bond between a Norwegian Forest Cat and its humans is very strong and deep. Of course, no cat should be punished by its humans, but with the Norwegian Forest Cat, negative responses to punishments will probably appear more quickly and intensively than with other breeds. The desire to please you in this case would result in your cat becoming withdrawn and developing even more behavioural problems. For this reason, you should avoid all forms of punishment and berating.

You will find that, because of its high intelligence, your Norwegian Forest Cat will react very quickly to the combined "no-yes" method. It learns very quickly that certain behaviour results in disadvantages for it and that the alternatives are better. Using of this method consistently, you will achieve your aims very quickly with most cats of this breed.

HOW TO TRAIN YOUR CAT TO BE ALONE

If you have to work and regularly need to leave your kitten for several hours each day, it is important to train them to be alone. Some cats have no problem at all being alone. Others do not like it at all, but with the right training it is possible that they will be able to endure it.

The simplest method is to get yourself a second cat but this is not suitable for everyone. If this is true in your case, you must ensure that your cat has enough ways to occupy itself. In many cases where an owner has asked me for help, it has been pure boredom which has led to the behavioural difficulties. If otherwise well-behaved cats suddenly stop using the cat litter and start marking the couch, it could be a call for help. Your cat is perhaps trying to tell you that it is bored and urgently needs a change.

It is exactly this which you should avoid from the beginning. You have read in the previous chapter how to furnish your home so that it is suitable for cats. You have also learned about the cat cinema. This is top priority for cats which are kept in the house all the time. Make sure your cat has the prospect of watching interesting things through the window while you are away.

You can also turn your home into a little adventure centre. There is no limit to your imagination here. Try not to offer the same things every day but ensure there is a little variation from time to time.

One day you could give your cat a feed ball which it can amuse itself with for hours in order to get to its well-loved treat. Balls dangling from places or cuddly toys can act as alternatives. A cardboard box to chew up is also a wonderful toy for many room-tigers.

One small tip – something my kitties love – is the use of scented cushions. I fill a small fabric pouch with mint and hide it in the flat (for example in small cardboard boxes or underneath the cat blankets). By leaving these things around the home during the day, I offer the cats an exciting game of hunt the treasure.

Make sure that the water bowls are always full when you leave the house. You should also make sure the litter box is clean and if not, clean it.

You should never leave a small kitten on its own for many hours at a time. You will need to train it to get it used to the new situation. Start with just a few minutes. When you see that this causes no problems you can slowly lengthen the time you are away. Show your kitten that it is not in danger and that you will always return. Unfortunately, there is no special plan for this, as reactions can be very different, depending on the character of your Norwegian Forest Cat.

You are probably wondering how long you can leave your kitten alone and when you can start with it.

As I mentioned at the beginning of this handbook, I suggest taking a few weeks' holiday to start with. You should not be leaving your kitten alone for long periods of time right from the start. Start leaving it for short periods at a time in the second week and increase it at the speed which your kitten can cope with.

You can leave some kittens alone for several hours after about four months, some after three and others after six. The rule of thumb is that pure house cats, living without other cats, can be left alone for about 4 – 5 hours. After that period of time, someone should look in on them, feed them and play with them. If you are unable to look in on them during your lunch break, because of the constraints of your job, you should look around for someone to do it for you. Perhaps a neighbour would be willing to do this?

Cats who enjoy the company of other cats can also be left alone for a whole day. However, at the first sign of "wild urination" and scratching, you need to make sure that your cat has a big enough variety of activities to keep it occupied.

Be aware that your cat will probably want you to make good the hours which you have been away, once you come home.

It will shamelessly play on your bad conscience and will want to be spoiled and entertained.

Is it not wonderful when someone is so happy to see you?

Special Characteristics of your Norwegian Forest Cat

Remember how human-orientated and playful your Norwegian Forest Cat is. I urge every owner of this breed to seriously consider getting a second cat – your cat will appreciate it.

If this is not possible for any reason, I ask you to do these two things:

- Try hard to get someone to look in on your Norwegian Forest Cat, to feed it and play with it.
- Be creative and think up new ways to make your cat's day interesting. If you cannot satisfy its need to be entertained during your absence, you will need to offer enough other alternatives.

How to Understand Cat Language

In order to make raising your cat a success from day one, it is important that you and your Norwegian Forest Cat speak the same language. Your little four-legged friend does not care about the words you say, it pays attention to the tone of your voice and your body language. For this reason, you need to send the right signals. In time, you will learn below how to do that.

It is quite simple, really: If you want your cat to pay attention to you, always speak in a happy, interesting voice. If you want your Norwegian Forest Cat to be quieter, adjust your voice and move slowly and quietly. Never raise your voice and shout at it.

Cats are very sensitive to our moods and know, without shouting and screaming, if we are annoyed. Shouting and screaming lead to your cat being afraid of you and avoiding you. You do not want that, do you?

Even more important and more complicated than interpreting your signals seems to be the interpretation of cat language. I hear people complaining all too often that their own cat is even harder to interpret than all the others. This could be true but not because the cat is not giving signals but because the owner has never learned to understand them.

Naturally, each cat has its own particularities when expressing itself, but there are many general messages which the majority of Norwegian Forest Cats send out and are generally understood. I would like to list these for you now.

On the following pages, we will look at what you can deduce about the mood of your cat, by looking at its tail, ears, eyes, whiskers and general posture:

Let us start with the **tail** as it is not only there to help balance it. It is one of the most important methods of communication between cats. The most common are as follows:

- The tail is raised and the tip of the tail is facing forwards: This is an open, friendly signal. Your cat is saying "hello" and showing that it is self-confident. The lower the tail sinks, the less self-confident your cat is.

- A straight tail, almost horizontal to the floor: This position is considered neutral. It can mean that your cat is assessing the situation and has not yet made up its mind. In this pose, you should definitely pay attention to the other body signals.

- The tail is tucked in between its legs: This is a sign of great fear. Your cat is panicking and you need to find out what the reason is and get rid of the cause as soon as possible.
- The hairs of the tail are standing on end: Your cat has reached an extreme situation and is not far from flying off the handle. This could have defensive or offensive reasons. Either it will take to flight or wildly storm its prey or opponent.
- The tail begins to quiver in a strange way: I have learned that this quivering is a sign of happiness and excitement. You should see this as a great sign of acceptance if your cat behaves in this way when it is near you.
- The tail whips from right to left and back again: This is a warning signal that your cat will shortly change into a form of defensive or offensive behaviour. If you are currently petting your cat, you should stop immediately otherwise you will soon have its claws in your hand. If the tail is jerking, this could be out of irritation or frustration. You should find out what is bothering it.

You will probably find more variations in your cat as I could only mention the most important and common forms of behaviour here. Keep an eye on any variations in your cat and remember them.

Now we come to the **ears** - the position of the ears can tell us a lot about the mood of your cat. Did you know that your cat can move its ears independently of each other? It takes more than 20 muscles to be able to do that. Of course, your cat is able to convey a great number of moods, using its ears. You will find the three most important ones below:

- The ears are standing straight up and forwards: Your cat is paying attention to its environment. When your cat relaxes, it moves its ears slightly outwards.
- It is pinning its ears back: If the ears are only slightly pinned back, your Norwegian Forest Cat is nervous but is trying to take in more information. If the ears are pinned back completely, it is getting ready to attack. Generally, you can assume that the closer its ears are to its head, the more nervous it has become.
- The ears move independently of each other: Your cat is investigating. Perhaps it does not know itself as yet what to think about the situation. Pay attention to the rest of its body language and notice any changes.

Now we come to the **eyes.** Even a cat's eyes can tell you a lot about how it is feeling. Here are a few examples:

- The pupils are dilated: Dilated pupils can be due to the bad lighting. However, it may suggest that your cat is in fight or flight mode. The dilation of its pupils enables your cat to be able to sense its environment better and be aware of possible dangers. If you notice that its pupils dilate suddenly, you should definitely watch out for other body signals.
- The pupils are narrow slits: This is the opposite to having the dilated pupils and suggests that your cat is in a positive mood. Generally, you can assume that it is relaxed and contented.
- Your cat is staring at you: This is a sign that your cat is ready to attack and wants to challenge its prey or opponent. Try to create a diversion, many cats can switch over and react to the new circumstances.
- Your cat is avoiding your gaze or that of others: It is signalling that it is not interested in a confrontation.
- Your cat is blinking slowly: If your cat is blinking at you, this is a very positive sign. I have often seen that it is a signal of great

> love. For this reason, I have got into the habit of blinking slowly at my cat when greeting it. You should try it!

Apart from signals coming from the eyes, ears and tail, taking notice of its **whiskers** will also help you to understand your cat better. Of course, a cat's whiskers are there, first and foremost, to collect information. If they are hanging loosely downwards, your cat is very relaxed and content. The more they are lying flat against the head, the more nervous your cat is feeling (it is trying to make itself small). Forward leaning whiskers can say many things. Initially, it suggests that your cat is trying to gather more information, but it could be showing interest in something or is, in fact, very inquisitive about something. However, it can also mean that your cat is preparing to attack and is collecting the last pieces of information it needs. Forward facing whiskers can also mean that your cat suspects danger.

You can see how complex understanding body language can be. It is important to take the context and accompanying signals into consideration when trying to interpret them.

Now we come to the most obvious method of communication – **general posture.** Cats will also let you know how they are feeling, using their body language. I have made a summary of the most striking positions below:

- Halloween posture: With that I mean that your cat arches its back and its hair stands on end. This has the effect of making it look bigger than it really is. As soon as you see this posture, you should hear the alarm bells ringing as this could mean that a storm is coming. Your cat is ready to defend itself with every method available to it.
- Crouched dwarf posture: Your cat is making itself as small as possible. The ears are pinned back and the tail is tucked in. It is sending the signal that it is not interested in fighting and does not want to look threatening in any way. However, if it feels cornered in any way, it is more than ready to defend itself.

- Rolling cuddle cat: When your cat is happily rolling around on the ground, this is mostly a positive sign. It is saying that it is very friendly and harmless. In young cats it is an invitation to play. In older cats it could mean that it is being defensive because there is no better proof that the inner-predator of your Norwegian Forest Cat trusts you than showing you its unprotected belly. But do not make the mistake of thinking that this is an invitation to stroke its belly. Many cats do not like to be stroked there at all. You can either enjoy this sign of love from a distance or stroke its head gently.

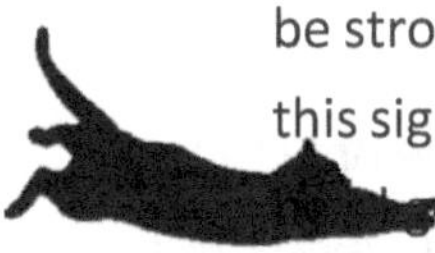

- The Sphinx: Your cat is lying relaxed with its paws stretched out before it. There is hardly a more relaxed and contented posture than this. If the eyes are also slightly sleeping, your cat is feeling well at that moment.

I hope I have been able to give you an insight into the ways in which a cat communicates. A cat will not bite or scratch without sending out a warning signal first, even if it is sometimes very subtle for some human observers. Now you know the subtleties, you will probably be more aware if your cat's eyes suddenly dilate or its tail begins to whip, and you will know that it is probably time to stop whatever you are doing.

Special Characteristics of your Norwegian Forest Cat

There is no breed-typical body language. The only thing I can suggest to you is that you need to learn the individual body language of your Norwegian Forest Cat. I am only able to describe the most striking characteristics but there are still so many nuances!

Take your time and learn how your kitten communicates with you, from the first week onwards. Pay attention to the position of its ears, how its tail moves and watch its eyes. How does your cat appear when it is relaxed and what exactly did it do, shortly before it suddenly scratched you?

Learning the body language of your own cat is one of the most interesting things about getting to know each other

EXCURSUS: WHY CATS DO NOT REALLY LIKE BEING STROKED

People tell me all the time that they are frustrated that their cat does not like to be stroked and ask how they can change that. In reality, it is a fact that cats have highly sensitive sensory receptors all over their bodies, particularly in their back regions. Even the slightest touch of the skin or hair can cause intense over-stimulation which can lead to the cat scratching or biting.

Many cat owners have to get used to the idea that most cats (there are some exceptions) do not like being cuddled, particularly on their bellies.

I always suggest stroking only the head and back of sensitive cats. Cats tend to have a higher tolerance to that before they feel over-stimulated. However, every cat is different and it is important that you find out how your particular cat likes to be petted.

Here are a few general tips for you which are well accepted by most cats:

- Never make the mistake (particularly with cats which you do not know) of simply stroking a cat! The cat always has to come to you. Of course, you can meet them half-way by gently stretching an arm out with the forefinger pointing towards it.

- After that you just have to wait to see if the cat touches your forefinger.
- If it gives you a nudge with its nose (which, by the way, is the normal greeting between cats) you can go ahead and gently stroke the bridge of its nose with your finger.
- If the cat likes it, you can extend the stroke to its cheeks, chin and forehead.
- If the cat is still looking very relaxed – and only then – you could try stroking over its shoulders and beyond.
- Advanced petters could give a gentle ear massage. Take the ear tips between your forefinger and thumb and make circular movements to the ear. You will need to experiment to find the correct pressure and speed. If you are able to find the optimum combination, you will make your cat very happy.

- Chapter 5 -

THE MOST IMPORTANT TRAININGS

You have come this far. On the pages to follow you will discover how you can take the first steps towards training your little Norwegian Forest Cat. All the following tips are based on the principle of positive conditioning, which I have already mentioned. Your cat will learn that it is rewarded by showing specific behaviour and will be happy to repeat it for you if you ask it to do so.

All the methods listed below are, in my opinion, essential for your cat to lead a happy life. Unfortunately, I keep seeing examples of owners not taking notice of the needs of their cats, resulting in extreme behavioural disorders. In order that this does not happen to you and your Norwegian Forest Cat, in the following pages you will learn how you can train it to come to you when called, how to feed it properly, how to get it housetrained and how to get it used to the transport box.

Before we start with the individual training methods, I have a few tips for you to ease the way:

- Always start your training just before it is time to feed your cat. This has the advantage that it is hungry and that there is a feed at the end of the exercise, which will feel like a jackpot.

- It is completely acceptable to feed your cat treats as a reward. Only few cats will be happy to work with you with just a little praise (after all, they are not dogs!). You should have some especially tasty treats ready for the more complex exercises. However, if your cat has carried out a command or exercise successfully, it is sometimes enough just to give it a little praise.
- Always do your training in a quiet room and make sure there are as few distractions as possible. Once your cat carries out the commands correctly, you can plan in the odd distraction.
- Cats love routines. For this reason, it can be helpful to do your training in the same place at the same time.
- Do not overtax your cat with the training, these can be challenging times for your cat. I recommend spending about 10 to 15 minutes per training unit. Ideally, you will want to finish the training with a successful exercise (i.e. one which is carried out

correctly). You should make sure that it is you who finishes the training, not the cat who leaves you, bored, in the middle of an exercise. Watch its body language and try to find the right moment to finish.

- Get used to using fixed commands. Always say "here" for example and not sometimes "come" and sometimes "come here" etc. Your cat does not understand the individual words you say but it can recognise specific sounds and remember that a specific sound means that it is supposed to come to you. If you keep changing the command, you will confuse your cat and destroy the success you have achieved during training.
- Never try to teach more than one new exercise at a time. This can also confuse and overtax your cat. Take them one at a time and begin with the new one when the old one has been fully mastered.

At the end of this chapter, I will give you some more tips on how you can deal with unacceptable behaviour. These include problems with biting and scratching, being a nuisance, destructiveness, soiling and fear of everyone and everything. The method is basically always the same. This could help you to deal with further problems you may encounter which are not covered in this book.

LEARNING ITS OWN NAME

Teaching a cat to understand its name starts much earlier on than most people believe. It begins with the choice of the name. My first tip is:

Choose a name with only two syllables!

Why? Your cat is not able to recognise a long name. A shorter name can be confused with “here” or “sit”. If the real name of your cat is longer, choose a shorter nickname for it.

Researchers have discovered that cats can recognise names with high-frequency vowels, such as “i” and “a” better. These can also be identified from a greater distance.

Hissing sounds, such as “s” and “z” or “sh” sound very unpleasant to cats and it is better not to use them in a cat name. It is thought that this stems from the sound made by their former archenemy, the snake.

Starting proper training with the name should begin in a relaxed atmosphere. Wait for a situation where your cat is feeling very much at ease. Say the name in your cat’s direction. As soon as it reacts, reward it. A reaction could be a lifting of the head. If it looks at you as well, all the better. As soon as your cat reacts in this way, it is your job to give it an immediate reward. My preference would be in the form of a treat.

Show your cat that its name always means something good. Repeat the exercise and reward it when you see the reaction.

An addition to this exercise is to ensure that your cat links its name to many happy moments. For example, if your kitten likes to come and cuddle on the couch with you in the evening, use this intimate moment and repeat its name when you stroke it gently down its back. Make sure that you do not say too much else and do not combine its name with other words.

At feeding time, you can call it by name or say the name as a form of greeting when you come home. If you follow these tips, I am sure that your kitten will soon begin to react positively to the sound of its name.

Finally, I have a warning for you: Make sure that you do not use its name in a negative way, either at the beginning or at any other time. If your cat has behaved badly (because it knocked down your favourite vase from the shelf, as an example) you should never shout its name loudly. You should only use the name in a positive way. If you use it for negative behaviour too often, it will link bad experiences to its name and not react to it as you would like.

COMING ON COMMAND

As soon as your cat has learned its name, you can start teaching it to come to you. I recommend every cat owner to continue practising this until it is perfect, because it is most important, for both you and your cat, that it comes back to you when you call. There might be a time when it is necessary for your cat to come to you when you call and failure to do so could have serious consequences.

How to you construct the exercise?

I suggest calling the name of your cat first, in order to draw its attention to you. In most cases your cat will look at you. As soon as you get eye contact, you give the command "here" and offer it a particularly tasty treat at the same time. Start off a small distance away and, when your cat comes to you, you give it a lot of praise and of course the treat.

Now repeat the exercise in a different place.

Keep repeating this exercise over and over again. If it is successful, you can begin to increase the distance. You have achieved the supreme discipline when your cat comes to you when you are one or two rooms away.

What do you do if your cat will not comply?

My first tip is always to increase the motivation. Make sure that your cat is really hungry then it will run to you for the treat. If you have a very hard nut to crack, you can begin to use its food as a training tool. By this I mean that it must come when it is called before you give it its food. This may sound harsh but remember that your cat is used to hunting for its food. Coming when called is easy compared to that.

Sometimes it can be helpful to change the treats. Perhaps they were not tasty enough.

Finally, I would like to end with a similar warning as before: If something negative is waiting for your cat when it comes, only call it if it is an absolute emergency. It is very important that your cat does not associated something negative with coming to you. For example, if you want to cut its claws, never call it – always go and find your pet.

Special Characteristics of your Norwegian Forest Cat

Because your cat is very affectionate, you will very probably have no problems at all with this exercise compared to owners of other breeds.

If you and your Norwegian Forest Cat enjoy this exercise, you can go a step further and try some retrieval training, or perhaps even go for a walk on the lead. Anything is possible with this breed and serves to intensify your relationship. However, as this is not part of the basic program which every cat should learn from the start, I am not going to explain it here in any more detail.

FEEDING CORRECTLY

Feeding your cat is one of the most underestimated processes in the life of a cat. I am always surprised how little thought some people give to this important part of their cat's life. Often, food will be crudely piled into the bowl, or there is always a filled bowl in the kitchen – or even worse: There is a food automat.

Feeding is one of the most intimate moments in the daily rhythm of your Norwegian Forest Cat, which you should not only enjoy but consciously create.

My first rule is:

Never put out your cat's food for it to eat round-the-clock. Remember the inner-predator. Is it used to having food whenever it wants, or does it have to hunt for it? Can you seriously imagine that it is helpful for the self-confidence of your cat, to be able to help itself to food whenever it wants? (Apart from the fact that the food goes stale over time.) If you do that you will destroy all the success you have had during training and, at the same time, be working against your cat's natural instincts.

For me, set meal times are not negotiable. In the wild, your cat would be used to eating small portions of food several times a day. We should orientate ourselves to this rhythm.

For example, you could feed your cat when you have just got up, then when you come home from work and lastly just before you go to bed.

These times are particularly good because it is exactly at those times that your Norwegian Forest Cat will experience an increase in its energy level. If you remember what you have learned earlier in this book, you will know that the basic needs of your cat are as follows: hunting – catching – killing – eating – resting.

Putting food down only satisfies a fraction of the basic needs of your cat. I have already suggested that you play with your Norwegian Forest Cat several times a day, it is a good idea to play with it shortly before feeding time. In this way you can go a long way towards satisfying the natural instincts of your little predator. Let it become part of your daily rhythm to play extensively for about 10 - 15 minutes before every meal (much less with a young kitten). You will be delighted to see how happily your cat will respond and how enthusiastically it will devour its food.

This brings us directly to the next subject. Cats devour their food. They hardly chew, they just swallow everything straight down. Sometimes you can watch how your cat will shake its head while it is eating – that is its inner-predator. If you think your cat is devouring a little too much, there are slow feeder bowls available on the market. You can find them in pet shops or make one yourself by placing a few clean stones into the feeding bowl.

Some cats gulp their food down so quickly that they later have to vomit. What you see in the vomit is almost exactly the same as what was in their bowl. If this persists regularly, despite using a slow feeder bowl, you should perhaps find out if there is a physical reason for it, such as hypertrophy.

Many cat-owners tell me that their little kitties are very fussy eaters. I usually find that the problems with fussy eaters are usually down to the owners themselves. Firstly, I suggest not leaving food down all day (that is one of the main causes!). If your cat always has access to its food, it is often not prepared to try out anything new. Sometimes it is difficult to distinguish between a fussy eater or one which is simply not hungry. If your cat does not eat all its food, take away the rest immediately. Do not leave it standing in case your cat wants to eat later, or you will teach it to be fussy. Get your little kitty used to eating at regular times, right from the beginning and teach it that it cannot save some for later.

Here are some more tips on how to motivate your cat to eat:

- **Flat plates:** Often, the food is not the reason why cats eat too little or too much, it could be the bowl. Cats intensely dislike their whiskers touching the edges of the bowl while eating. Give your cat its food on a flat plate or shallow bowl instead.

- **Mouse Temperature:** Cats do not like their food too hot or too cold. Particularly wet food, which comes directly out of the fridge, will not exactly cause a storm of enthusiasm. Try to serve the food at "mouse temperature". Your cat's inner-predator will love it
- **Consistency**: Some cats prefer a particular kind of consistency in their food. Some love solid chunks while others prefer paste or pellets. Offer your cat a variety of consistencies right from the beginning and notice which it likes best.
- **Variety of Flavours**: Try various flavours occasionally. Get it used to not having the same thing on its plate three times a day, right from the beginning. Instead, open its world to the diversity of flavours. The earlier it learns that food does not always taste the same, the less chance there is that your cat will refuse to eat a new food.
- **Choosing the Feeding Place:** Choose the feeding place with care. Remember that

cats do not like to feel cornered – they always need more than one escape route. Do not put the food directly next to the litter box (should be obvious) but also not directly next to its water bowl. Make sure that your cat gets some peace to feed, particularly where small children and pets, such as dogs, also share the house

- **Special Wishes:** Cats are very astute and learn very quickly that they can get their special wishes fulfilled with a "meow". The best way to avoid this is not to start it in the first place. You decide what it is fed and your cat can either decide to eat it, or not. Never react to your cat meowing special requests – if you do that, it is your own fault.
- **Sickness:** Learn to understand your cat so well that you can see the difference whether it is not eating because it is being fussy or if there is something physically wrong with it. If it is the latter, you should consult your vet relatively quickly.

You should consult with your breeder or animal shelter as to how often your kitten should be fed at the beginning. You will normally receive all the information you need and, that way, you can avoid the trauma which a change in food could cause for your cat.

HOUSE TRAINING

It was the year 1947 when Ed Lowe invented cat litter. With this simple invention, he revolutionised the relationship between the cat and the human. From that day onwards, people accepted their cat doing its business in small boxes inside the house, leading to a drastic reduction in living space for the cat, and people began to spend much more time with them.

Within a very short time we have come to expect that cats must modify their natural instinct (of doing their business wherever they want to, thereby marking their territory) for the sake of cleanliness and order. The problem of house-soiling is one of the most common things which requires us to take preventive action. After all, nothing makes us more angry than when our little kitty urinates on our favourite cushion.

Happily, most cats learn to use the litter box very quickly. Kittens from reputable breeders, which have been well socialised, have usually copied their mothers and learned to use the litter box. If your kitten is not ready for that, I have a few tips for you as to how you can solve this little problem relatively quickly:

Make it easy for your cat to use the litter box. This means you should put the litter box somewhere which you think it is probable that it will relieve itself. This is always the case, just after your cat has eaten or after waking up. Watch your little Norwegian Forest Cat carefully and carry it quickly to the litter box when it crouches and lifts its tail.

This is very laborious at first, but will lead to quick results. Once your kitten is placed on the litter box nearly every time from you, it will soon be looking for the box when it feels the need to do its business.

Remember never to scold your kitten if it has an accident. Your cat will not connect your scolding to the accident, so you can save yourself the trouble. Clear it up without comment and continue as normal.

As I previously mentioned, you should start by using the same cat litter that your breeder (or animal shelter) has used and make sure that your kitten can enter the litter box without difficulty.

It is most important to choose the spot where the litter box will go very carefully in order to avoid problems in the future. I know that they are not very decorative and never look good in a living room or bedroom, but this is exactly where they belong. You are most often in these rooms and they smell strongly of your scent. It is in your Norwegian Forest Cat's nature to want to leave its mark in those places.

Offer it the possibility of using that nice clean litter box, placed next to the bed or sofa.

Below you will find some further reasons why some cats often avoid the litter box and what you can do about it:

1. **Too little choice**: It is not enough for your cat to only have one litter box. You need at least one more. It is not natural for them to use only one place to do their business. They prefer different place for their small and big businesses.
2. **Put them in separate places:** Do not make the mistake of putting the little boxes directly next to each other. They belong in strategically important rooms, which are used most often by you and smell strongest of your scent.
3. **Room fresheners:** Cats do not only use their litter boxes to relieve themselves but also to leave a mark which serves to reinforce their domination over their territory. Do you think it will be helpful to put a room freshener directly above the litter box? I can understand that you do not wish to have unpleasant smells in your home, but doing that will ensure that your cat will not use the litter box, thereby

rendering it useless. The same applies to perfumed litter.

4. **Too much of the good stuff:** Who does not know the expression "the more the merrier"? This does not apply to cat litter. Many cat owners fill the litter boxes much too full and many cats do not like that. Particularly long-haired cats, like your Norwegian Forest Cat, do not like their hair to touch the cat litter (remember the many receptors in the hair follicles). I recommend only putting 2 to 5 cm of cat litter into the box for a start, then try out what your cat likes best.
5. **Too small:** It is not only the height of the litter box that can be a problem. Often it is the length too. Your cat needs to feel well and it is important that it can turn comfortably in it. I suggest a minimum of one and a half lengths of your cat's body. Ask the breeder how big the mother cat is in order to get the correct size right from the beginning. Generally, Norwegian Forest Cats need a litter box which is bigger than most owners would like.
6. **Too hidden:** Cats do not like to stand in places without a second exit. Put the litter

box in the most open places that you can. The same applies to litter boxes with tops. No cat likes to walk into a trap. Do not buy a litter box with a top, or if yours already has a top, take it off. Try not to put it in a place decorated with flowers, figurines or anything like that. Such things would almost certainly stop your cat from using the litter box.

7. **Too dirty:** Cats do not like to use dirty litter boxes – no great surprise for an animal which spends most of its day preening itself. I often see litter boxes which have not been cleaned for days. Even though it may sound obvious, I will say this once again: You must scoop the litter boxes once a day. However, going to the other extreme is also not helpful. There are owners who completely empty and disinfect their cats' litter boxes every day and then are surprised that their cats urinate all over the place. You have to understand that, for the Norwegian Forest Cat, the litter box is a place to leave its mark, so the box has to smell of the cat. Cleaning it too much will backfire on you. It is perfectly reasonable to completely empty and wash out the litter

box with hot water once a month. Please do not use soap, your cat will not like the smell. It is sufficient to rinse out the box with hot water if you remove the soiled parts with a small scoop every day.

If your cat is not using its litter box, go through the above tips one at a time and check if there are any problems for your Norwegian Forest Cat. If you cannot see any and nothing else has changed to disturb its rhythm, you should consult a vet to rule out any physical causes.

USING A TRANSPORT BOX

Every cat owner should take his cat to the vet regularly for check-ups. It is particularly important for your kitten as it probably needs a few vaccinations. As very few vets make home visits these days you must find a way to take your cat to the vet and this is where using a transport box comes in.

However, you can make the first mistake before you even buy one. You need to ensure that your box is big enough for such a big and heavy cat as the Norwegian Forest Cat and that it can carry a weight of up to 9.5 kg. The box should be made from hard plastic so that your cat cannot scratch or bite into it.

In addition, the box should have two openings. The door at the front should ideally be one which your cat can use to routinely go in and out of. Once you have arrived at the vet, cats are often less than cooperative. If this is the case, a removable lid is worth its weight in gold. The lid can be opened by the vet and the cat can be removed without problems.

Some cats are calmer if the box is covered up with a cloth during transport, but you should ensure that the cloth is not too heavy so that your cat can breathe well. This is particularly important in warm weather. Air vents in the side of the box would also be helpful here.

The dearly-loved wicker basket is not very popular with most vets. The reason for this is that the cat can dig its claws very effectively into the weave. In addition, there is usually only one opening in them. This results in the vet being unable to take the cat out of the basket. The cat finds itself feeling cornered and harassed if the situation continues and it can only get worse. Finally, plastic boxes are easier to clean.

If you want to make your cat more comfortable in the transport box, you can put a blanket or a cushion in the bottom. Even better, if you put a t-shirt inside which has been worn by you, the scent can help your cat to remain calm. Remember that everything can become soiled during transport.

How do you get your cat used to the transport box?

If you have a kitten, you are lucky that it has probably not had too many bad experiences in the transport box. Ideally, it has no particular feelings about it one way or the other.

Put the box in a room (the living room, for example) and lay a used t-shirt and a blanket inside. Now you need to wait. How does your cat react to the box? Sooner or later, it will want to explore it and it is then that you have to act. Praise it and give it a treat. Show it that the box is a wonderful place. You could use it to play games.

If your kitten does not explore the box on its own or has already had a bad experience with boxes, you can try bribery. Throw a treat into the box from time to time. Every time your cat eats the treat, throw the next one inside, and so on.

Never push or lift your kitten into the box. Allow it to make the decision to explore the box. I know that it can sometimes take longer than you would like, but believe me, it will be well worth it down the road. If you have a particularly apprehensive cat, it can sometimes help to remove the top and allow your cat to get used to just the lid.

Once your kitten has accepted the box as a place to rest and sleep, then comes the next step. Show it that it is not a problem when you close the door, for example at the next feed. Give your cat its food in the box. Close the door during that time and open it again. You can close the door for short periods when the cat is lying relaxed in the box. Then begin to extend the time slowly in short steps.

As soon as your cat has remained calm when you close the door, you can test how it reacts when you lift the box. Be very careful and watch its body language carefully. Use treats as encouragement and reward. Once the lifting part has been successful, you can try walking a few steps. This will probably take a lot of your patience and you will need a lot of repeats. Get your cat used to being carried around in your home with the box closed for short distances.

Once you have accomplished that, we can take a step further. Next time, carry your cat into the car. Do not start the engine, allow it to look around for a few minutes and then take it back into your home. Repeat the exercise until your cat feels comfortable and calm in the car. The next step is to turn on the engine and perhaps travel a metre forwards and backwards. How did your cat react? Keep the time that you have the engine running short so that your cat can gain experience and will not be overstressed by it.

When your cat has got used to the running engine, you could drive once round the block. Do not be afraid to give it plenty of treats so that your cat remains calm and experiences something positive connected to the journey.

If you think your kitten is overstretched by the experience, you should stop doing the exercise and start again the next day a step further back. Do not try again with the failed step until the previous step works without problems. It can be helpful to tire your cat out with an exciting hunting game before trying it again, so that it is a little more relaxed.

I know that the process seems to be very long and you will probably consider jumping a few steps. Think hard about it before you do so! If your cat has had one single bad experience with the transport box, it will be much harder for it to get over that than it would be to take the time to get it used to the box, slowly.

One final tip: Once your kitten has got used to the box, you should not only use it to go to the vet. Take little trips with your cat so that it does not make the connection between the box and the vet and all those examinations and nasty injections.

Special Characteristics of your Norwegian Forest Cat

When your Norwegian Forest Cat is fully grown, it will be a large, heavy cat. For this reason, you will need a large, stable transport box, the bigger the better to make your cat feel most comfortable.

Your cat needs to move around a lot so it really does not like being locked up in a transport box. You will need to take the adaptation phase very seriously, slowly taking one step at a time. Try to keep the box time as short as possible.

Their closeness to their humans is very strong which makes the trick with the worn t-shirt work particularly well, calming your cat – I can only recommend it. Never use your favourite shirt as it is probable that it will not come back from a visit to the vet in good condition.

AVOIDING UNWANTED BEHAVIOUR

Cats are not machines! Sometimes they will behave in ways we do not approve of. Surprisingly, the cat is not usually at fault for the bad behaviour, it more often lies with us– the owners.

On the following pages I will give you some tips on how you can avoid most of the problems. You will quickly realise that the cure is often to use the no – yes method. If there is a form of behaviour which you do not like, try to make it unattractive for your cat. Never forget to analyse what the need is behind the bad behaviour and offer an alternative for it that your cat will prefer.

Here are the problems which we will be concentrating on:

- My cat is always biting and scratching
- My cat is always getting on my nerves
- My cat is destroying my furniture
- My cat will not use the litter box
- My cat is very nervous.

At the end, I will give you a few useful tips to deal with other problems, which often occur.

BITING AND SCRATCHING

Anyone who lives in a house with cats will unavoidably bleed at some time or other – that is unavoidable. However, it should be the exception rather than the rule. If you notice that your cat is keeping its distance from you or vice versa, or that you or your friends describe your cat as a "demon" because it bites and scratches everything and everyone coming too close, it is high time to do something about it – of course, it is better to start doing something about it before it gets that far.

During this difficult time, you should remember: Cats are not evil and do not naturally tend towards bad behaviour or even hate. Normally there is a reason for it and there have already been signs (which are mostly unnoticed by us humans). No cat scratches or bites unless it feels it is the only path left to it. It is important that you remember that you want to be a team again and this is only possible if you keep an open mind about your Norwegian Forest Cat and have not already given up on it.

The first thing to do is to rule out any physical reasons for your cat's behaviour. For example, is it always aggressive if it is touched in a particular place? Or have you noticed anything which could suggest an injury or sickness? If so, you should consult your vet immediately. Sometimes cats can be aggressive because they are suffering a lot of pain and cannot tell us about it.

If your cat is healthy, you have to become a detective. I recommend keeping a detailed diary (perhaps for a week). Describe exactly when your cat is aggressive and what exactly happened. Keep to the facts and describe the incident as if you were an independent detective. Make a note of the exact time preferably including a sketch of your home and exactly where it happened. Include where and how long you have played with your Norwegian Forest Cat. Be precise and, after a week, look at your notes where every interaction has occurred.

Have you noticed anything? Do the attacks always occur in the same place (e.g., at the window or under the table) or perhaps at the same time (e.g., when you arrive home from work)? These are all clues which can help you find out what exactly is behind your cat's behaviour.

<u>If the attacks always happen at the same time:</u> Everything points to your cat being a pure energy monster at that time and is close to exploding – which it shows through scratching and biting. In most cases it is the time when you are most active and have a lot to do. Many people find it difficult to find enough time in the morning to play with their cats. However, if your Norwegian Forest Cat shows its aggressive behaviour exactly at that time, it is your duty to find at least 15 minutes to play a hunting game (hunting – catching – killing – eating – resting). You must give your cat

a valve to get rid of its overflow of energy. If you do not do this, you will have to put up with the scratching and biting.

<u>If the attacks always happen in the same place:</u> This could mean that your cat is projecting its aggression towards you. If it happens mostly at the window, it is possible that it has been watching free-running cats outside and is reacting aggressively to that. Because your Norwegian Forest Cat cannot reach the other cat, it unloads its aggression on the first person it can reach, which is probably you. Try to avoid other cats from entering that area (using a better fence, water pistol, sound alarm etc). In this case, your cat is feeling that its territory is being threatened and the only thing you can do is to remove the competition from its view.

If your cat is aggressive when it is under the table and you or someone else walks by the table, this has a very different cause. If this happens, the inner-predator of your cat has become active. It has found a safe hiding place and watches as its prey walks by. In that case, I recommend not playing with your cat in the middle of the room, but start it under that table. Show your cat that you approve of its hunting behaviour but offer an alternative to your ankles.

You will notice that play is really not a luxury but a necessity, just like going for walks with a dog, a cat needs to play several times a day. Its need to hunt – catch – kill – eat –

rest is innate in all cats. If you do not give it an outlet, your cat will look for one – and you will not always like it.

Sometimes the problems with biting and scratching are home-made. Kittens often use hands to play with. A sweet little kitten will hit your hand with its paw and we think it is cute. However, when an 9.5 kg cat does it, it appears aggressive. How should your Norwegian Forest Cat know that what it was allowed to do as a kitten is no longer allowed and how does it know what it is not permitted? It cannot! For this reason, I am warning you never to use your hands as a toy and certainly not as prey. Everyone in the household and of course visitors will need to comply with this unwritten rule.

Another home-made problem is over-stimulation. We have already spoken about cats becoming over-stimulated if they are stroked wrongly or for too long. This usually results in the use of its claws and teeth. As soon as the body language of your cat tells you that it no longer wants to be stroked, you must stop immediately. This can even happen after just a few seconds. If you do not stop, it is your own fault if you get scratched or bitten.

Finally, I recommend that you get your cat's claws trimmed regularly, then it hurts less. Remember that you should never react by berating or punishing your cat. It will not understand why you are doing it and this could cause a great deal of damage to your relationship. Let it go and suffer it without showing too much emotion. I know that it is not always easy but nobody suggested it would be.

Special Characteristics of your Norwegian Forest Cat

Your Norwegian Forest Cat will grow to become a large cat, so it is particularly important that you never use your hand as a toy. Apart from that it is your Norwegian Forest Cat is very active and its energy level climbs very quickly – more quickly than other breeds. Watch out for the signs and react immediately.

You should notice as early as possible if there is a problem with aggression and begin the detective work immediately. The larger the cat, the bigger and deeper the wounds.

ALWAYS GETTING ON YOUR NERVES

Who has not lived through it? You want to have a moment to relax and read the newspaper but your cat is jumping on your lap, the table or is constantly meowing until you give it some attention. Or your cat declares that night is day punctually at 3:12am and starts throwing books off the shelf.

Do not these moments make you livid?

Quite honestly? I can understand you but I also understand your cat. Its behaviour is in most cases a desperate attempt to stave off its boredom.

In order to get a grip on the situation, we will start by doing the detective work and keeping the diary as previously described. Describe everything that you notice and where it happens and of course when you played with your cat and where. Do you recognise a pattern? Does your cat always get on your nerves when the energy level of the family is increasing? Again: Ensure that you make playtime part of your daily routine, preferably always at the same time.

If your cat is throwing things on the ground, it could be just an accident. Does your cat always throw pictures off the mantlepiece when it is trying to get to the window? Or the muesli pack from the fridge when your cat wants to be with you at breakfast time? Analyse the situation, say no to unwanted behaviour, offer an alternative.

Now we come to the biggest source of anger: Your cat will not let you sleep at night, hopping on the bed, meowing for hours or scratching at the door. Sleep deprivation awakes the darkest side of us and the behaviour awakes cravings in our cats which are not good for our relationships.

The first thing you need to make clear to yourself is that, despite widespread opinion, cats are not active at night. They sleep at night, just like we do. However, it is true that they are very active at dusk. With the right training you can get every cat to sleep normally at night. Waking up at night is not the price you have to pay because you have chosen a cat as your pet!

How do you go about it?

Let us start, as always, with food. Always feed your cat at least one hour before you go to bed. What should you do before that? Correct! You should give your cat a good game of hunting – catching – killing – eating – resting. Allow yourself a lot of time, make your cat tired and then play another game (this time a short one). After that comes the food, then your cat will probably preen itself and then fall into a long, deep sleep.

You should teach your cat to be active when everyone in the household is active (so that there are corresponding energy levels). Once you are all awake, your cat will gather its energy and you must give it an outlet to get rid of it again. The same applies to the quiet times: When you are quiet, your Norwegian Forest Cat should be too.

Now we come to the greatest challenge: Ignoring. It will probably take about two to three weeks where your cat will still wake you up, even though you have kept to the previously mentioned tips. You have to be strong during this time and ignore everything your cat does. Never give it the satisfaction of drawing your attention to the behaviour. I know how hard these two weeks will be, but it is worth it.

Finally, I would like to say a few more words: Most cats who get on their humans' nerves, are suffering from acute boredom. Try to put yourself in the place of your cat and analyse what it does during the day. Can you give it more variety in its hunting – catching – killing – eating – resting phases? What about the cat cinema? Is your home designed properly for cats (with cat walks, sufficient cat trees etc.)? Are you using the no – yes method?

As hard as this may sound, the majority of bad behaviour is caused by us humans and not by our cats. They are just behaving normally according to their needs. If we are not able to satisfy their needs, this will result in some form of misbehaviour.

Special Characteristics of your Norwegian Forest Cat

Your Norwegian Forest Cat is very attached to humans and active. This usually leads to it getting on your nerves a great deal if it does not have the feeling it is getting enough attention. It will creep around you constantly, sit in front of the computer screen or television and makes sure that it gets your attention.

When you have such a sensitive cat, it is most important that you spend enough time with it. You must make it part of your routine to play with it intensively, particularly in the mornings or when you come home. While you are playing with it, you will need to give it your full attention. If you have one hand on your smart phone or are watching television out of one eye, you are not paying full attention to your cat and it will notice that.

DESTRUCTIVE BEHAVIOUR

Do you know cat owners whose couches are completely scratched and who have to replace their mattresses regularly?

As I mentioned in a previous chapter, scratching is an important necessity for your cat. It does not destroy your furniture out of malice, nor because it wants revenge. It is easy to come to this conclusion because the destruction is directed mostly at your favourite things. But now you know that scratching is a self-confident sign of your cat marking its territory and that it will automatically choose places where your scent is present – that is mostly the couch or bed.

You should not stifle this compulsion but what you can do is to steer it in the right direction. You should never accept that you, as a cat owner, have to put up with scratched couches, as this is not the case. Yes, cats have to scratch, but not specifically on your sofa, bed or couch table.

As always, the combined no – yes method works best here in solving the problem. Begin by making an intensive analysis: Why is your cat scratching? When does it scratch? Which surfaces does the cat prefer? How safely does it stand? How big is the scratched surface?

Compare this information with your existing cat trees. Where do they stand? What material are they made of? How big is the scratch surface? How safely does it stand? Does it wobble when your cat wants to scratch on it? That alone drives many cats to look for something more robust, such as a solid-standing sofa. Compare your cat tree with the object which your cat prefers to use. Let us assume that it is the sofa. Try to find a cat tree which is more similar to your scratched sofa than the one you have now.

The next step is to stop your cat from scratching the sofa. As you know by now, you do not have to shout "no" at it, you can do it in a much better way. See to it that the sofa is no longer interesting for the cat. You could use double-sided tape or aluminium foil. Both of these will spoil your Norwegian Forest Cat`s fun. Because these are only temporary solutions, you need to offer your cat a suitable alternative, which brings us to the new cat tree.

Put the tree as close to the sofa as you can. This is where you spend the most time and your cat is closest to your scent. Ensure that the new cat tree stands firmly and is big enough. Measure how far your cat can stretch upwards. I recommend that the scratch surface should be at least 15 to 25 centimetres longer than that. The base should measure at least 50 x 50 centimetres.

The last step is to make the new cat tree attractive for your cat. Do not force it to use the tree, do not lift it onto the tree or rub its paws on it. That will not achieve anything, in fact it will probably have the opposite effect and your cat will avoid it immediately.

Many owners use catmint to make new objects interesting for their house-tigers. However, it has been my experience that the scent of the owner works much better. Rub the new cat tree well with a used t-shirt or towel. Integrate it into your next hunting game and reward your cat with treats when it gets close to, or even uses it. Use positive reinforcement so that your cat learns that the new tree is something good and that using it brings rewards (as opposed to the sofa, which your cat keeps getting stuck on at the moment). As soon as your cat associates positive experience with the new cat tree, you can slowly reduce the number of rewards you give it and eventually stop giving them altogether. You should keep the preventive measures to your couch for a short time after that, then slowly remove them.

Special Characteristics of your Norwegian Forest Cat

Your Norwegian Forest Cat loves to jump and play, so it is imperative that your cat tree is stable. If, as a young animal, they discover that the cat tree wobbles, over time this could culminate in your cat avoiding the tree altogether and using the sofa instead. A stable tree is the most important thing for such athletic cats.

Norwegian Forest Cats, which are not receiving as much attention as they need, will scratch the couch, walls or furniture in order to be noticed. They have learned from experience that they will get the attention they want by baring its claws in the presence of the owner. If you have analysed that your cat mostly scratches something when it is close to you, I suggest that you spend more time occupying it. This could be a cry for help against acute boredom – which happens quicker with this breed of cats than with other, more relaxed breeds.

SOILING PROBLEM

Honestly: In almost ninety percent of cases, I am asked what owners can do about the constant urination problem with their cats. There is hardly another subject which causes such despair and aggressiveness as the soiling problem.

Contrary to the destructiveness from the previous chapter, the soiling problem is not usually a sign of self-confident territory marking, but insecurity, stress and lack of self-confidence.

If I have done a good job up to now, you will be in possession of all the tools you need to fix the problem alone. However, this concerns a problem which can lead very quickly to frustration and a feeling of helplessness, so I am giving you a few tips to help with that. It is important for you to know that every cat is an individual, every home and every family is different. This makes it very difficult for me to give you general solutions, but I will try to give you tips and show you clues as to how you can tackle your own problems.

Before you continue, you should look back a few pages. In the chapter called “House Training” I listed 7 of the main reasons why cats could be avoiding the litter box. I would suggest checking those first to make sure that none of those situations are present before reading on, as in many cases you can resolve the problem the way I described.

If the problem lies elsewhere, you will have to return to doing an intensive analysis. When and where does your cat urinate in your home? Make yourself a map and mark each time it happens for at least a week. Also make a note of what happened directly before it.

There are usually three reasons why your cat does not use the litter box:

- The first is territorial stress. Your cat is anything but self-confident and compensates with over marking. The threat could be real or imagined, but your cat is definitely not feeling masterful over its territory.
- There could be a health aspect to your cat not wanting to use the litter box. If you have the smallest suspicion that something is wrong, you should speak to your vet about it.
- Lastly, it could be the litter box itself. In this case your cat is not avoiding the litter box for strategical reasons, but because it does not feel comfortable using it. This could be the result of an earlier trauma, the composition of the litter box or litter, its positioning etc.

Using your knowledge and making your own analysis, bearing in mind the place of the "crime scene", you can begin to make some assumptions. Below are a few examples:

- Your cat regularly urinates in your bathroom: Irrespective of whether it has urinated in the bath or wash basin, this behaviour shows that your cat has developed a strong aversion to its litter box. Perhaps the entry is too high, the box is too small or – most probably – it does not like the litter. Try out a different kind of litter and/or get a new box.
- Your cat likes to urinate on your personal things: This behaviour is not malevolence but a call for help. Your cat is suffering from acute territorial stress. Try to find the cause of that stress. If you live in a household with several pets, is it possible that your cat is being mobbed? Is there a new member of the family, new partner or have you just moved homes? Think about what could have caused the stress of your cat. It has to be your top priority to reduce the stress (possibly going back to using the base camp) and get it used to your new partner, the baby or the new surroundings.

- Your cat prefers to urinate on your favourite piece of furniture: This is also caused by territorial stress as these pieces of furniture are loaded with your scent. Sometimes, it can help if you move the litter box directly next to the furniture in question. However, researchers think there could also be other causes, such as those mentioned in the previous point. You should try to strengthen your cat's self-confidence, by playing a lot with it, several times a day.
- Your cat urinates (sprays) outside walls, doors and windows: The reason once again is territorial stress, but this time it is probably directed against outdoor cats. It should be your main priority to ensure that these outdoor cats do not come near the house and particularly not close to the window. Your cat will continue defend its territory, by leaving its own scent in these places, until you have removed the threat. Leave your cat's own scent right next to its markings, perhaps using a cat tree or litter box. This will ensure that its scent is always prevalent and will make additional markings unnecessary.

- Your cat often urinates in the middle of the room, under the table or chairs: This behaviour also suggests territorial stress. Your cat is feeling threatened and wants to keep everything in view while urinating. You must strengthen its self-confidence at all costs. In addition, you could take another look at where you have put the litter box. Are its exits blocked? Could your cat feel as if it is in a trap? Change the position of the litter box and avoid using a lid. If there are other animals living in the house (such as dogs or other cats), you must ensure that your cat is not mobbed when using the litter box or becomes trapped.
- Your cat always does its business right next to the litter box: In this case your cat is probably showing its dislike of the litter box or there could possibly be health reasons. You should get your cat checked over by a vet. It knows that it is supposed to use the litter box but something is definitely wrong. Your cat is trying to get as near the litter box as possible. If it is an antipathy against the box itself, you should definitely try changing it for another, also try changing

the litter you are using. Make various trials, each for a good length of time as everything points to the fact that your cat simply does not feel comfortable using its litter box.

If these tips have not helped you, I have a few final questions to ask you, which can often lead to solutions. Always ask yourself: When did the problem start and what changed shortly before it?

Did you change something with the litter box, the location, material, environment or litter? Find out what is bothering your cat about the new situation and change it back again.

Did something change in your rhythm? Have you just started a new job? Is there building working going on outside your house? Do you have a new hobby? Analyse everything which may have changed the amount of time you spend at home or which has changed in your household. Norwegian Forest Cats love routines and if too much changes at one time for it, it reacts by showing symptoms of stress. Find out what is causing it and try getting your cat used to the new rhythm, ensuring at the same time that all its needs are being met.

Is there a new person in your life? New people (or animals) can change your cat's world more quickly and profoundly than you think. Most owners do not realise that cats are usually more sensitive than dogs. Be very gentle when introducing new people or animals into your environment. There should be no sudden or unprepared encounters. The best way to do that is to get your cat used to the new person or animal by linking it with something positive (e.g., scents placed close to its food bowl) before the first meeting. Once you have done this, I suggest pressing the reset button and starting again from the beginning. Your cat and your new partner do not have to be the best of friends, but they can learn to tolerate each other. That is the most important thing for you.

Finally, here are some absolute taboos: Never lift a grown cat and carry it to the litter box. Do not put its excrement in your pet's face or lock it in a small room with its litter box until it finally uses it. Yes, I have seen all this happening and none of it has led to the desired behaviour. Neither screaming at it nor punishing it will do any good, so save your energy. Clear up and be done with it.

Special Characteristics of your Norwegian Forest Cat

The importance of the size of the litter box and the amount of litter inside it is very often underestimated. It sounds so simple, but often (if there are no other reasons for it) your problems will be solved by getting a bigger litter box. If your cat also no longer sinks in so deeply that its fur touches the litter, it is completely satisfied in its new litter box.

The location of the litter box is just as important for the Norwegian Forest Cat breed. It is very people-oriented and because of this, it prefers to do its business close to us. I know that this is not particularly pleasant, but for your cat it is a way to show its love. Always check the location and ask yourself if it is well chosen for your Norwegian Forest Cat.

AFRAID OF EVERYTHING AND EVERYONE

Dealing with anxiety is the supreme art, and anything but simple. You must be aware that you have to take very small steps to alleviate anxiety. There is no magic solution and each solution is individual to each cat as the reasons for the fear are very diverse.

It is very difficult for me to help you here if I do not know what is causing the anxiety in your particular cat. However, so that you do not feel left completely alone with your problem, I will give you a few examples of how to deal with your Norwegian Forest Cat's anxiety in this chapter. I have chosen the two most common causes of anxiety: The big pain of separation and the constant creeping away and hiding.

Separation pain is something that many people do not associate with cats. There are countless manuals which deal with this subject for dogs but people always say that cats do not form a close relationship with their cats, so that you seldom find any literature on that subject. However, the fear is present and happens more often than many think. Some cats show their anxiety by nervously following their humans around in the mornings before they leave the house. Some develop a compulsion to clean their fur or mark the bed or couch and others drive the neighbours mad with their constant meowing.

We need to analyse the situation before we take any corrective measures. Cameras in the house are extremely useful in dealing with separation pain. Watch how your cat reacts when you leave the house and when the "problem behaviour" begins. Make detailed notes.

After that, the work begins for you. Begin by often leaving the house for short times. With particularly anxious cats, this could be for just a few seconds. The important thing about this exercise is the repetition. Ideally, you will leave your home 15 – 30 times a day and return after a short while. This way, you are signalling that you are going away is not so bad. You should ensure not to make a fuss when leaving the house. Do not say goodbye when you leave or greet when you return. You should just ignore your cat completely. I know that this is not easy but it is the central element in combatting anxiety. If you make a fuss when saying goodbye, you are encouraging it to become anxious, your cat will sense your bad conscience (and believe me, it will) and it will assume that something bad is coming. Also, the more prolonged your greeting is when you return, the longer your cat will be waiting for you at the door. Is that what you want? Or would you prefer your cat to spend the time, relaxed instead of standing by the door, waiting for you to come home.

You are probably asking yourself how long you have to do this exercise, are you not? A long time! You will not be able to dictate the speed of the progress because it depends solely on how well your cat is doing. You can slowly increase the lengths of absence (at your cat's speed). You should also try not to be too predictable. Do not always leave the house at the same time using the same routine (e.g., shoes on, jacket on, take keys and goodbye). Put your shoes or jacket on in between, so that your cat does not only associate it with you leaving. Get your keys occasionally, but do not leave your home.

Before you leave the house for any length of time, you should play a long game of hunting – catching – killing – eating – resting with your cat. I know that particularly in the morning there is very little time, but if you want your cat to feel better, there is no better alternative. It has two advantages for your cat: The first is that the playtime inspires the inner-predator in your Norwegian Forest Cat. Cats who have problems with being alone are seldom in balance with their inner-predator. Through intensive play before being left alone, you will strengthen that part of your cat. Eating is the second advantage. Giving your cat food will create a diversion so that you do not feel it necessary to say long goodbyes.

Have a good look at what you are offering as a cat cinema. Will your cat have enough entertainment while you are out of the house?

This brings us to the next example problem of your cat constantly creeping away and hiding. It often feels like there is not a cat in your house at all, because you seldom see it. In this case, you have got yourself a classic scaredy cat and you will have to teach it that the world has a lot to offer.

Once again, the first step is the analysis. Make a note of where your cat is spending its time. Where does it go to hide? Which room is it using? Where does it have the courage to go?

Let us assume that your cat spends most of the day under your bed and only comes out, tail between its legs, for a short time and within a 2-metre radius around the bed. If this is the case, I recommend marking the radius on the ground with a crepe band. This has two advantages: On the one hand, you are making clear to yourself how small the world of your Norwegian Forest Cat really is and on the other hand you know where you have to start.

The very next day, put its food bowl exactly on the line and pull it a very small distance further out from the circle every day. Only extend the perimeter by centimetres each day. If you feel it is too much for your cat, let the bowl stand on the same spot for a day or two before moving it again. This way, you extend the comfort zone of your cat, little by little. You may find it useful to mark your progress by placing crepe band strips on the floor, so that it is easier to assess.

As soon as you see the first signs of progress, you can begin to close off its sanctuary by blocking off the most difficult to reach corners, as this is probably where your cat spends most of its time. Our example is the bed. You should never block off the whole sanctuary at once. Proceed slowly, a little each day, until the whole area is no longer accessible.

It is important that your cat does not suddenly find itself with nowhere to hide, so you will need to provide adequate alternatives for it. A cat bed or cat cave is a very good solution here. You could place a used (by you) t-shirt on the bottom, so that your Norwegian Forest Cat will accept it more readily.

Another important component in dealing with scaredy cats is play. Cats which are so frightened, as in our example, have great problems with their self-confidence and they do not often meet their inner-predator. We need to change that and you can do that best by playing hunting games with it. You know by now that this brings your cat's inner-predator out best.

This means for you: You must play much more with nervous cats than you would do with self-confident ones. If you cannot do it any other way, you may need to start the games under the bed. Your aim would be to tease the cat out from under the bed during the game.

Once your cat is out from under the bed, you should try carefully taking the game closer to the comfort line that you have marked. Your top priority is to encourage your cat to step over its comfort line without it noticing.

During play, your cat concentrates on its prey and the innate self-confidence of its ancestors emerges, then it will start to behave differently. Even the biggest scaredy cats can turn into self-confident hunters. Use these moments of self-confidence to extend your cat's world, slowly but surely. In this way you can take the fear out of the unknown room and link it to positive things. Bit by bit, your cat will begin to use its newly discovered environment when you are not playing with it or feeding it.

You need to be aware that this is a very long process which is not over in one or two weeks. We are speaking more of months, even years. If your cat is not only fearful, but is suffering from a chronic anxiety disorder, it is possible that you cannot free it from that condition alone. If that is the case, I strongly suggest consulting a vet or animal psychologist. No general tips can help you here, you will need to let the professionals look at it and work out a therapy with you.

How can you recognise an anxiety disorder? Your cat will draw away from everyone more and more, it will become unclean, hardly purrs, does not play and is very nervous. All of those are symptoms of a chronic anxiety disorder. Of course, you can try all the things I suggested first but if they do not help, there is no alternative to visiting a vet or animal psychologist. The aim of the treatment would be to restore and strengthen the bond between you and your Norwegian Forest Cat and build up its self-confidence. Once this has been achieved, the fear will slowly subside.

Tips for reducing anxiety towards visitors

If your Norwegian Forest Cat is always creeping away when visitors come, this suggests that it is suffering from an acute anxiety disorder. If this is the case, there are several things you can do to try and resolve it:

- Tell your visitors in advance that they should not ring the bell but let you know of their arrival by telephone. As many cats are afraid, even hearing the doorbell, this is one way to avoid one anxiety factor.
- Leave the house (closing the front door behind you and re-enter together with your visitors.
- Ask your visitors to ignore your cat. They should not look at it, walk towards it or speak to it. All those things can feel threatening to a scaredy cat; therefore, it is a proven means of reducing anxiety.
- Your visitors should remain quiet, meaning they should not talk too loudly or wave their arms about too much.
- If it is feeding time while the visitors are still there, your visitor could take over the feeding. The idea is that your cat will link something positive with the visitor (visitor

= food = good). If it is not feeding time, your visitor could offer your cat a special treat. You can give it to your visitor before entering the home and let your visitors give the treat to your cat. The visitor should not give your cat the treat directly after entering, but after the cat has had a little time to get used to the stranger.

- Ensure that your cat has enough places to withdraw to in the room where the visitor will spend most of the time. These withdrawal places should be high up, so that your cat can watch the stranger in the house from a little distance.
- Play with your cat close to your visitor, this will strengthen its self-confidence and make a positive link.

General Tips

Finally, I have a few general tips for you. Below you will see a list of the most common problems which I am regularly asked about:

- **Your cat enjoys harassing the visitors who have the most fear of cats or does not like them. It leaves other visitors alone.**
  This behaviour is typical for cats. So-called cat-lovers will probably give your Norwegian Forest Cat more attention than it really wants. For this reason, your cat will avoid the contact with your visitor, particularly if it feels as if it is being watched. However, if a visitor does not like cats or is afraid of them, this tends to awaken the cat's interest and motivates them to investigate further.
- **Your cat will not drink out of its bowl, but prefers running tap water:**
  Some cats do not like standing water. It is not common but it is difficult to change a cat like that. If you have such a cat, I suggest buying a cat fountain as you will probably not find a better solution. Offer your cat an alternative to the water tap so that your water bill does not rise too extremely.

(Remember the combination no – yes method)

- **Your cat does not like your new partner:** Cats show us clearly when they do not like something. This unfortunately includes humans. If your cat is prone to extreme behaviour (e.g., urinating on clothes or even people), something has gone wrong during the introduction phase. They will probably never be the best of friends, but we can see to it that your partner and your cat can tolerate each other. Firstly, you should place a t-shirt, previously worn by your partner, next to your cat while it is eating. This way you will establish a positive link between eating and the scent of your partner. In the evenings, when you are petting your Norwegian Forest Cat on the sofa, you could also slip on one of your partner's t-shirts. Your Norwegian Forest Cat should link all the positive things to the scent of your partner. At the same time, your partner should ignore your cat as much as possible and in no case force themselves on it. If you always use the partner scent training, (and do not forget to swap over the t-shirts from time to time –

the scent should always be fresh) your cat will learn at least to tolerate your partner and possibly even more.

- **Your cat has climbed a tree and will not come down:**
  Do not panic, it is not a reason to call the fire brigade or start climbing ladders yourself. It is true, anatomically, that a cat can climb better upwards than downwards, but they can always come down if they want to. Just have patience. When it is hungry at the latest, it will climb down.
- **Your cat is always climbing up your curtains:**
  Here you can also use the combined no – yes method. Make climbing up the curtains unpleasant for your cat. Either you can use the double-sided sticky tape method, or fasten the curtains so that they fall down easily. Remember to offer your cat a suitable alternative. Why is it climbing up the curtains? Does it want to reach a window or shelf? If so, place a cat tree in a strategically suitable place and praise your cat enthusiastically when it uses the tree rather than the curtain.

- **Your cat has chosen an unsuitable place to sleep in (like, for example the wash basin, linen basket or washing machine):**
  Use the combined no – yes method once again. Make the spot unpleasant to sleep in, but offer a worthy alternative.
- **Your cat always uses the same plant pot as a cat toilet:**
  Firstly, check if there is a problem with the available litter box. If not, make the use of the plant as a cat toilet uninteresting. One useful method is to cover the whole pot and the earth with aluminium foil, as cats do not usually like the texture of aluminium foil. Lemon peel also works wonders, but do not forget to offer your cat an alternative. One possibility is to swap over the position of the plant and the litter box.

- Chapter 6 -

CHECKLIST FOR THE START

There is a lot to think about when your cat is about to move in, particularly if your Norwegian Forest Cat is your first cat. I have made a few checklists, which you will find below, so that you do not miss or forget something and so that nothing will stand in your way of getting off to a perfect start.

There are a lot of things for you to watch out for, so that you and your Norwegian Forest Cat will live happy cat and human lives. You should check over the list several times to make sure you have not forgotten anything.

What will you learn here?

Firstly, I will give you the most important things to deal with before you even decide whether or not you want a kitten. Once you have made that decision, I will tell you what to watch out for when buying your cat, which formalities you will have to deal with and what should be on your shopping list for the start. Finally, I will list the things you need to consider so that the environment will be safe for your kitten and that nothing bad can happen to it.

PRELIMINARY CONSIDERATIONS

Before you decide to bring a Norwegian Forest Cat into your life, there are few things you need to consider. This should be done before you decide to buy a kitten, so you can offer it a happy life and one which is appropriate for its kind. If you are not sure that you can answer all these points honestly and without reservation, it would be better to wait a little before taking the plunge so that you have more time to make the necessary arrangements. A Norwegian Forest Cat is not a cuddly toy but a living creature!

- ☐ Are you prepared to spend the next years looking after a cat in the appropriate way?
- ☐ Is your current home the right place for a Norwegian Forest Cat? Remember that you will be getting a big cat which needs more space than some others.
- ☐ Is your present lifestyle suitable for life with a cat? (i.e., Your work, holidays, social environment etc). What will you do with it if you are away for any length of time?
- ☐ Do you feel able to take care of your kitten as it is shown in this book, so that you can both live happy lives? Are you strong enough to withstand those sweet eyes and

be able to say no if necessary? (and it will often be necessary)

- ☐ Do you have enough time every day to take care of your Norwegian Forest Cat, play hunting games with it and spend time with it? Remember that you have chosen a particularly playful breed. Time could be critical here.
- ☐ Are you able to afford the costs of purchasing the basic equipment, food, vet costs, insurance etc.?
- ☐ Have you checked if someone in your family has an allergy to cat hair? Countless cats end up in the animal shelter each year because their owners have not paid any attention to that situation.
- ☐ Have you decided who will take over the main tasks within the family, and is everyone in agreement?
- ☐ Have you checked with the landlord (if you have one) whether cats are allowed in the building? Check your lease to be on the safe side.
- ☐ Are you physically fit and healthy enough to be able to care for a Norwegian Forest Cat for the whole of its life? You need to think at least 15 years into the future.

- ☐ Are you aware that your cat will bring a fair amount of dirt into your house and leave hair everywhere (and I mean everywhere!)?
- ☐ Will you be able to take care of your Norwegian Forest Cat round the clock at the beginning (even at night)? Have you made a plan how to do that in the first few weeks?
- ☐ Are you happy with the idea that you will have to share your home with several litter boxes, cat trees and catwalks? Remember that you cannot put those things in the cellar or broom cupboard because it needs to be exactly where you and your family spend most of your time. Your home will never look like it did before.

BUYING YOUR CAT

Many mistakes are made before or during the purchase of the cat, which people later regret because they have been instrumental in supporting illegal cat breeding. In addition, there are certain things to consider to find the right cat for you and make a good start.

- ☐ Have you gathered enough information about the Norwegian Forest Cat as a breed; researched the breeders in the internet and found a reputable breeder (or shelter as an alternative)? This handbook is only one of various sources to get the information you need.
- ☐ Have you thought whether you want a male or a female?
- ☐ Have you thought of a name for your little rascal? Remember the tips in this book!
- ☐ If you are buying your cat from a breeder, there are several points to consider:
    - How do the kittens look and how do they behave?
    - Is the mother present and is she looking after her brood?
    - Is the breeder offering other breeds? (Not a good sign!)

  - Is the kitten living in a clean and suitable environment?
  - Is the breeder asking you questions about how it will be living; does he seem interested that the kitten will be going to a good home?
  - Is the price realistic or unexpectedly low? (The latter could be a sign that something is not right.)
  - Did you receive detailed information about feeding over the next few weeks etc.?
  - Is there a written contract of sale with the most important information about the breeder, liability issues, sales price, handover, pedigree etc.?
- ☐ If you are getting your cat from an animal shelter you should take the following into consideration:
  - What is its history? Have there been any trauma or sicknesses?
  - Is anything known about its parents and/or previous owner? (Sicknesses, behavioural disorders, etc.)
  - How has the kitten developed since it has been in the shelter?

   - Did the kitten develop any special relationships with other animals?
   - Which requirements do you have to fulfil to be able to adopt the kitten? (Yes, some shelters do not just give away the animals but want to be sure that they will be better off after the adoption.)
   - Remember to ask about feeding for the next few weeks. The animal shelter should be able to give you detailed information about that.
- ☐ Have you planned to make several trips to the breeder/shelter to find out if you and your Norwegian Forest Cat are suited to each other?
- ☐ Are you allowed to take a blanket or toy to the breeder/shelter so that the animal can get the scent of its new home?
- ☐ How will you transport your new companion from the breeder/shelter to your home? Has your Norwegian Forest Cat ever travelled in a car or used a transport box before? Do you have something to clean your car with (just in case)?

FORMALITIES

You will have to complete various formalities and paperwork before you can take your kitten. This is important so that no bad (and expensive) surprises happen later on. These are the most important things to watch for:

- ☐ It is advisable to take out a third-party insurance for your kitten (in case it damages anything or injures anyone (for example if it is running free and runs in front of a bike and the rider falls).
- ☐ Check the legal requirements in your environment. Do you have to get permission from your landlord?
- ☐ Find a good vet. Research in the internet and ask for recommendations from your friends. Once you have found a good vet, check what vaccinations and check-ups your pet will need. If you are going to get your first cat, I suggest having a detailed conversation with the vet before you even get one. Most are willing to speak with you in detail about your future cat's health and nutrition. Many cat owners prefer vets which have separate waiting rooms for

dogs and cats in order to make the visit the least stressful as possible.

- ☐ Find an emergency vet for your Norwegian Forest Cat in case something unexpected happens (such as a sickness or accident). It is important that you find out before anything happens because once you have an emergency, you will not have the time or the nerves to find a suitable one.

SHOPPING LIST

You will need to get together a fair amount of equipment so that you can offer your Norwegian Forest Cat a good home. Unfortunately, this can quickly become expensive but it is unavoidable and needs to be done before your new companion moves in. I recommend having the following in advance of your new arrival:

- ☐ Food plate and water bowl (possibly with a stand with adjustable height). If your Norwegian Forest Cat is a food-gobbler, you may need to buy a slow feeder plate for it.
- ☐ A harness (take care to buy the right size) and a short lead for the kitten. You may be wondering what you need to use it for. My suggestion is not for taking walks, but for taking your pet to visit the vet. A harness and lead offers a little more safety in controlling your cat, should it start to panic.
- ☐ At least two baskets with soft linings to use as refuges.
- ☐ A transport box
- ☐ At least 2 litter boxes
- ☐ At least one cat tree for each room where your cat will spend a lot of time.

- ☐ A well thought-out catwalk system. You can use shelving for this. Entrances and exits need to be staggered with shelving or cat ladders. Cat trees are also very good entrances and exits.
- ☐ A birdhouse, insect hotel or wind chime for your cat cinema.
- ☐ A brush or comb.
- ☐ Toys.
- ☐ Food (the sort which your breeder/shelter has recommended) and of course treats.
- ☐ Door and stair gates to stop your kitten going into areas which it is now allowed to.
- ☐ Tick tweezers.
- ☐ Catmint.

SAFE ENVIRONMENT FOR CATS

You should ensure that your Norwegian Forest Cat has a safe environment to live in, not only to protect your furniture but also to avoid endangering your kitten. This includes the following:

- ☐ Decide which areas of your home are out of bounds and secure them, if necessary with door grilles. (My cats, for example, are not allowed in the sewing room)
- ☐ If you have a garden or balcony, ensure that it is escape-safe. Do not underestimate how small a hole your kitten can fit through! I recommend installing some kind of netting here too. This should prevent your Norwegian Forest Cat from escaping or coming to any harm. The net will also ensure that no bird falls prey to its hunting instinct.
- ☐ Fit child safety locks on all plug holes which your cat can reach. It may be necessary to fit them to your cupboard and drawer handles too – Norwegian Forest Cats in particular are very skilful with their paws and are quick to imitate.

- ☐ Hide all lose electric cables, you do not want your Norwegian Forest Cat to be nibbling at them – and it will if you do not stop it from doing so. If you are not able to hide the cables, you could think about getting some cable ducts.
- ☐ Take all breakables out of the reach of your cat and remove anything which it could knock over or which could fall. By that I do not mean putting such things a little higher – either you must put them in a room which your cat will not be going into or inside a cupboard. Believe me, when your cat is fully grown it will be able to reach anything it wants to.
- ☐ Make sure that you have blocked off any hiding places which you are unable to reach. I mean in particular places like under the bed, under the sofa or under cupboards. Make it impossible for your cat to go there, then you will never have the problem that your cat will stay there and not come out, or that you have to pull it out.
- ☐ Make sure there are no poisonous substances within your cat's reach, (such as

chemicals or poisonous plants) inside or outside in the garden.

- ☐ For the beginning, take away any carpets which could mutate to cat toilets. Only bring them back once you are sure that your kitten is house-trained. Start with one carpet and if that works without problems, you can bring back the next, and so on.
- ☐ Try to anticipate and remove any places which may be perceived as dead-ends. Make sure that your Norwegian Forest Cat can move freely around any large, open rooms. Take care to give it some places to hide at the beginning. Once your cat has gained some self-confidence you may be able to reduce the number of hiding places.
- ☐ Find a good place for the cat bed (not too far away from the family but in a relatively quiet place.

- Chapter 7 -

SUMMARY

Congratulations! You have taken a step which few cat owners are ready to take. You have taken the time to find out all about bringing up your Norwegian Forest Cat and because of that, you will have a much more peaceful and relaxed relationship with your cat than most owners.

You have discovered exactly what really counts:

- You know that training a cat is not impossible, but it depends on you alone whether it is successful or not.
- You have found out about the inner-predator, hiding within your cat, and that a housecat needs to let out that predator every day in order to be happy.
- You know that hunting – catching – killing – eating – resting is an important part of your cat's life and you must help it to satisfy that need several times a day. You know that play is not a nice optional extra but a daily duty, which

you must integrate into your daily plan right from the beginning.

- You have learned how to organise your home before your young cat even moves in. You have prepared your base camp; the litter boxes are laid out in suitable places and your cat walks are placed so that they allow your cat to move around above ground without knocking over anything from the shelves or misusing your curtains as cat ladders.
- You know that you must offer your cat some variety, so you have prepared exciting cat cinemas where it can make interesting observations of life outside from several different windows.
- You will bring up your cat lovingly and consistently because you know that berating and punishing it will not work. You have learned well the no – yes method and know how to use it. Firstly, you must analyse the situation and make a note of all the important factors. After that, you say no to the undesirable behaviour but offer your

Norwegian Forest Cat an alternative which will satisfy its needs equally well.

- You understand the body language of your cat, so that your actions do not lead to over-stimulation and you watch for the signs to avoid unnecessary scratching and biting right from the beginning.
- You know the most important points about raising your room tiger and have prepared it for its future life.
- You know that the number of rules you have made will not harm your Norwegian Forest Cat. On the contrary, it will help it to cope with its world. You have given it a home which satisfies its needs as far as possible and you have given it the security and leadership it needs.
- You will profit from the close and intensive relationship and relaxed atmosphere you have created with your consistent and loving upbringing. You will see that even those who ridicule the methods mentioned in this book will envy your relationship with your cat.

Finally, I have a few last tips for you:

Do not just read this book once. It is better to read it several times before your Norwegian Forest Cat moves in with you. It will not do any harm to refer back to this book whenever you need to, while beginning to raise your cat.

I need to remind you once again that this book is not a substitute for a visit to the vet or animal psychologist! Should you run into really big problems with your Norwegian Forest Cat – which I sincerely hope you will not – it is imperative to get the advice of a professional who can come to you and look at the problem with you.

I wish all the very best for you both. Above all, I wish you harmony, love and a long future together.

Cat Training Certificate

Congratulations! You have obtained all the knowledge necessary and are perfectly prepared to raise your Norwegian Forest Cat. With the right amount of attention and dedication you will enjoy many years of happiness together and will grow together as a real team.

I wish you both a lot of enjoyment!

____

Name of Owner

____

Name of Cat

_______________ _______________

Date of entry into home   Breed

Signed: Susanne Herzog

DID YOU ENJOY MY BOOK?

Now you have read my book, you know how to raise your Norwegian Forest Cat and how to build up a close relationship with it. This is why I would like to ask you a small favour. Reviews are an important part of every product offered on Amazon. It is the first thing that customers look at and often the review can make all the difference whether a customer buys the book or not. This factor has become even more important, bearing in mind the extensive choice of books offered by Amazon.

If you enjoyed my book, I would be very grateful if you could leave a review. How do you do that? Just click on the following button on Amazon's product page:

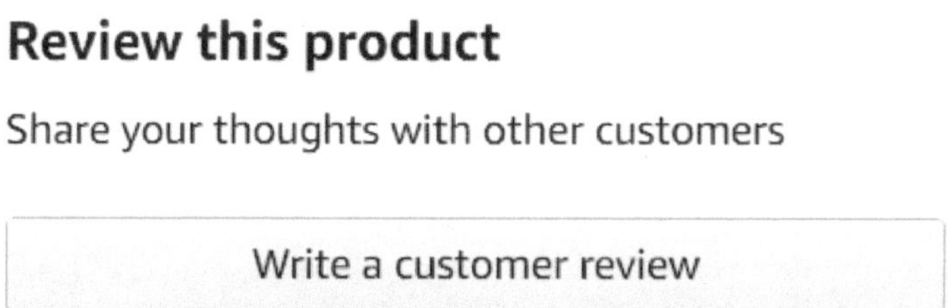

Describe briefly what you liked about it or how I can make this book even better. It will only take 2 minutes, honestly! You can be sure that I will read each review personally because I know that it will help me to further improve my books and tailor them to your specific wishes.

And with that I say:

Many thanks!

Your Susanne

BOOK RECOMMENDATIONS

Grab the second volume now and discover how to train and occupy your Norwegian Forest Kitten!

TRAINING A NORWEGIAN FOREST CAT – Guidebook how to train, occupy and play with your Norwegian Forest Cat

Cat training is often ...
» ... confused with the classical basic education of a kitten.
» ... only thought practical for particularly talented cats.
» ... thought of as being too difficult to do without any previous experience.

What difference does cat training make and what is it good for? And how can you and your Norwegian Forest Cat profit from it if you have no previous experience?
Do you sometimes have the feeling that your cat has too much pent-up energy and is not powered out enough, or perhaps it is bored? Then cat training is exactly the right thing for you. The simple but effective methods used in cat training will help you to tire out your Norwegian Forest Cat in a way which is compatible with its breed and, more importantly, have fun, while at the same time increasing the bond between you.
Satisfy your curiosity to learn background information, read reports on other experiences and obtain step-by-step instructions and insider tips which are tailor-made for your Norwegian Forest Cat.

Get your copy of this book today and find out ...
» ... how you can build up a unique relationship with your Norwegian Forest Cat and
» ... how you can power out your cat physically and mentally in a manner appropriate to its species.

Grab the third volume now and discover how to care and groom your Norwegian Forest Cat!

TAKING CARE OF A NORWEGIAN FOREST CAT – All you need to know about general cat caring, grooming, nutrition, and common disorders of Norwegian Forest Cats

Cat care is often ...

» ... underestimated and seen as unnecessary.
» ... reduced to fur care.
» ... completely neglected by many cat owners.

What does cat care mean and how do you feed your Norwegian Forest Cat correctly? How can you recognise disorders and parasites early or even prevent them?

If you want to know how and how often you should examine your Norwegian Forest Cat's eyes, ears, teeth, paws, fur and skin, this guidebook is exactly right for you. You will learn what you need to watch for. In addition, you will find out what you need to know about buying pre-prepared foods. You will discover the advantages and disadvantages of alternative feeding methods, such as home-cooked foods, as well as BARF, vegetarian or vegan foods. In addition, you will receive important information about the most common cat disorders as well as immunisation and castration, so that you can make good choices for you and your Norwegian Forest Cat.

Satisfy your curiosity and learn background information about your cat, read step-by-step instructions and insider tips which are tailor-made for your Norwegian Forest Cat.

Get your copy of this book today and find out ...

» ... how you can feed your Norwegian Forest Cat in a way which is both healthy and suitable for its breed
» ... how to examine and care for your cat and how to recognise disorders early

Get the new mandala coloring book now with 55 wonderful cat motifs!

MANDALA COLORING BOOK CATS - 55 animal motifs (cat theme) to colour-in for adults and children

Do you love colouring-in and are you very fond of cats? Perhaps you are feeling very stressed at the moment and need a moment to relax, a time to switch-off and enjoy your own company?

You can do that with this book. Inside, 55 hand-picked motifs of cats are waiting for you to bring them to life. Every picture is crafted with great care, creating a wonderful combination of animal drawing and mandalas.

While you are colouring-in, you will notice:

- how you can immerse yourself in the fantastic world of mandalas,
- how your body and mind come to rest and
- how you can leave stress behind you, through mindfulness and patience.

Immerse yourself in the world of mandalas and discover the 55 beautiful and individual cat mandalas contained in this colouring book. As if that is not enough, you will also receive additional 8 mandalas from the fantastic world of our colouring books – free!

Stimulate your imagination and enjoy a moment of peace and tranquillity, just for you!

SPACE FOR YOUR NOTES

REFERENCES

Dr. Brunner, David; Stall, Sam: Katze – Betriebsanleitung: Inbetriebnahme, Wartung und Instandhaltung; 1. Auflage, München: Goldmann Verlag 2015

Eilert-Overbeck, Brigitte: Unser Kätzchen – Was Katzenkinder brauchen; 4. Auflage, München: GRÄFE UND UNZER Verlag 2015

Linke-Grün, Gabriele: Wohnungskatzen – Wohlfühl-Basics für kleine Tiger; 8. Auflage; GRÄFE UND UNZER Verlag 2014

Ludwig, Gerd: Katze-Basics – Alles was Katzenhalter wissen müssen; 3. Auflage, München: GRÄFE UND UNZER Verlag 2015

Pfleiderer, Mircea; Rödder, Birgit: Was Katzen wirklich wollen; 4. Auflage; München: GRÄFE UND UNZER Verlag 2014

Hoffmann, Helga: Katzensprache – Kätzisch für Zweibeiner; 8. Auflage; München: GRÄFE UND UNZER Verlag 2014

Seidl, Denise: Katzenprobleme – Hilfe bei Aggression, Unsauberkeit und Angst; 1. Auflage; Stuttgart: Franckh Kosmos Verlag 2018

Ludwig, Gerd: Katzensprache – Schritt für Schritt verstehen lernen, 3. Auflage; München: GRÄFE UND UNZER Verlag 2016

Eilert- Overbeck, Brigitte: Katzen – Wohlfühl-Garantie für kleine und große Schnurrer; 4. Auflage; München: GRÄFE UND UNZER Verlag 2016

Galaxy, Jackson; Delgado, Mikel: Der Katzenflüsterer – Für ein glückliches Katzenleben; 2. Auflage; Königswinter: Heel Verlag 2019

Umgang mit Katzen: Anschaffung, Aufzucht, Ernährung, Erziehung, Pflege u. Behandlung in gesunden u. kranken Tagen, 5., neubearb. Aufl. / mit e. Vorw. [durchges.] v. E[ugen] Seiferle, zahlr. Zeichn. v. Roberta MacDonald u. 8 Photos auf Kunstdr. Taf., von Gay, Margaret Cooper, 1973

Katzen: unsere zärtlichen Freunde ; Anschaffung, Rassen, Abstammung, Erziehung, Pflege, Gesundheit, Zusammenleben, unter Beteiligung von Breuer, Antje, 1999

Katzen erziehen: der Katzenratgeber, mit dem Sie Ihre Katze verstehen lernen + zahlreiche Tipps zur Katzenerziehung, von Zerkel, Susanne, 2019

Unsauberkeit bei Katzen: Ursachen verstehen, vorbeugen und helfen, 1. Aufl., von Jones, Renate, 2013

Alles über Katzen: Haltung, Pflege, Rassen, von Gerber, Bärbel Bielfeld, Horst, 1983

Die Haltung von Katzen, unter Beteiligung von Deutscher Tierschutzbund, 2007

Katzen: Spielgefährten auf Samtpfoten ; [Tips für den Kauf ; Katzenhaltung und -pflege ; mit Katzen leben ; Lexikon der Katzenrassen], von Grau, Joachim, 1998

Hauskatzen: Kauf, Haltung, Pflege, von Nieser, Egon ¬[Verfasser], 1982

Katzen für Dummies, 1. Aufl., von Spadafori, Gina Pion, Paul D, 2004

Alles für die Katz: 88 Katzenspiele einfach selbst gemacht, von Heike, Grotegut, 2016

Die Katze lässt das Mausen nicht: 999 praktische und ungewöhnliche Tips für alle Katzenfreunde, von Szymkowiak, Margot, 1986

Das Hobbythek-Katzenbuch: Tips und Rezepte für gesundes Futter und natürliche Pflege, 1. Aufl., von Norten, Ellen; Pütz, Jean, 1997

Norwegische Waldkatze: Skandinaviens sanfte Wilde, von Ewald, Eva, 2015

Fall 24: 13-jährige Norwegische Waldkatze mit Fieber und Apathie, von Kiefer, Ingmar Trogisch-Hause, Antje Alef, Michaele Köhler, Claudia erschienen in Kleintier konkret (01.12.2017)

Waldkatzen: Maine-Coon Katze, Sibirische Katze, Norwegische Waldkatze mit Neva Masquarade und Türkisch Van, von Ortrun Wagner, 2009

Imprint

1st Edition

 Publishers: GbR Martin Seidel and Corinna Krupp, Bachstraße 37, 53498 Bad Breisig, Germany, email: info@expertengruppeverlag.de, Cover Photo: www.depositphotos.com.

Made in United States
Troutdale, OR
01/20/2024

17004915R00116